FIRST EDITION

Selected Readings
from the
World's Religious
Traditions

Tim J. Davis, Mark S. Bocija, Sue Burnam, Danya Furda
COLUMBUS STATE COMMUNITY COLLEGE

Printed in the United States of America
ISBN 978-0-9977857-9-1
1 2 3 4 5 6 7 8 JPS 21 20 19 18 17 16 15

Contents

1

Introduction to the Study of Religion

William James (1842-1910)

From Lecture 1, "The Varieties of Religious Experience"

James was an American professor at Harvard who sought to take an interdisciplinary approach to critically studying the various elements of human religious experiences. Following the path of historical-critical study of the scriptures in mid-nineteenth-century Europe, skepticism wrought by modern philosophers, and the birth of social science, his groundbreaking work, "The Varieties of Religious Experience," is derived from the Gifford Lectures on Natural Religion that he gave at the University of Edinburgh in Scotland, 1901-1902.

Objective Analysis of Religion

The next thing the intellect does is to lay bare the causes in which the thing originates. Spinoza (the seventeenth-century Jewish philosopher) says: "I will analyze the actions and appetites of men as if it were a question of lines, of planes, and of solids." And elsewhere he remarks that he will consider our passions and their properties with the same eye with which he looks on all other natural things, since the consequences of our affections flow from their nature with the same necessity as it results from the nature of a triangle that its three angles should be equal to two right angles.

Psychological Characteristics of Religious Leaders

There can be no doubt that as a matter of fact a religious life, exclusively pursued, does tend to make the person exceptional and eccentric. I speak not now of your ordinary religious believer, who follows the conventional observances of his country, whether it be Buddhist, Christian, or Mohammedan. His religion has been made for him by others, communicated to him by tradition, determined to fixed forms by imitation, and retained by habit. It would profit us little to study this second-hand religious life. We must make search rather for the original experiences which were the pattern-setters to all this mass of suggested feeling and imitated conduct. These experiences we can only find in individuals for whom religion exists not as a dull habit, but as an acute fever rather. But such individuals are 'geniuses' in the religious line; and like many other geniuses who have brought forth fruits effective enough for commemoration in the pages of biography, such religious geniuses have often shown symptoms of nervous instability.

Even more perhaps than other kinds of genius, religious leaders have been subject to abnormal psychical visitations. Invariably they have been creatures of exalted emotional sensibility. Often they have led a discordant inner life, and had melancholy during a part of their career. They have known no measure, been liable to obsessions and fixed ideas; and frequently they have fallen into trances, heard voices, seen visions, and presented all sorts of peculiarities which are ordinarily classed as pathological.

Often, moreover, these pathological features in their career have helped to give them their religious authority and influence.

> *James goes on to give an example by quoting the famous Quaker leader, George Fox, who tells the story of being called by the Lord to go to the city of Litchfield, England, to denounce the life and history of citizens there. In the middle of a snowstorm he was directed by God to take off his shoes and walk through the streets decrying the city and its Christian practice.*

Catholic writers are equally emphatic. The good dispositions which a vision, or voice, or other apparent heavenly favor leave behind them are the only marks by which we may be sure they are not possible deceptions of the tempter. . . .

Still, you may ask me, if its results are to be the ground of our final spiritual estimate of a religious phenomenon, why threaten us at all with so much existential study of its conditions? Why not simply leave pathological questions out? To this I reply in two ways: First, I say, irrepressible curiosity imperiously leads one on; and I say, secondly, that it always leads to a better understanding of a thing's significance to consider its exaggerations and perversions, its equivalents and substitutes and nearest relatives elsewhere. Not that we may thereby swamp the thing in the wholesale condemnation which we pass on its inferior congeners, but rather that we may by contrast ascertain the more precisely in what its merits consist, by learning at the same time to what particular dangers of corruption it may also be exposed.

Excerpts from this web edition of William James' "Varieties of Religious Experience" was edited and annotated for the World Wide Web by LeRoy L. Miller, tentatively entitled *New Age, New Thought: William James and the Varieties of Religious Experience*. This work is in the Public Domain. Introductory notes by Tim Davis (2016). https://worldu.edu/library/william_james_var.pdf

Emile Durkheim (1859-1917)

Elementary Forms of Religious Life

From *Elementary Forms of Religious Life*, translated from the French by Joseph Ward Swain, Hollen Street Press, George Allen & Unwin Ltd, London (1915). Introductory notes by Tim Davis (2016).

Emile Durkheim was a pioneering French scholar in the fields of sociology, philosophy, and social psychology. Along with Karl Marx and Max Weber, he is often credited with founding the academic discipline of social science. Durkheim has been called the "Father of Sociology". His ground-breaking Elementary Forms of Religious Life (1912) investigated various theories of religion and examined the cultural and social aspects of religious phenomena among both primitive and contemporary societies. Durkheim saw religion as one of the most basic functions of society, which at an early age, communally tied it together. He also suggested the human emotion was a primary factor in the religious experience, a response to a reality that was beyond our full comprehension.

Chapter I (excerpts)

Definition of Religious Phenomena and of Religion

I

One idea which generally passes as characteristic of all that is religious, is that of the supernatural. By it is understood that all sorts of things surpass the limits of our knowledge.

(pp. 24-25)

II

Another idea by which the attempt to define religion is often made, is that of divinity. "Religion," says M. Reville, "is the determination of human life by the sentiment of a bond uniting the human mind to that mysterious mind whose domination of the world and itself it recognizes, and to whom it delights in feeling itself united."

But there are great religions from which the ideas of gods and spirits are absent. . . .

(pp. 29-30)

Religious phenomena are naturally arranged in two fundamental categories: beliefs and rites. The first are states of opinion, and consist in representations; the second are determined modes of action. Between these two classes of facts there is all the difference which separates thought from action. . . .

By sacred things one must not understand simply those personal beings which are called gods and spirits; a rock, a tree, a spring, a pebble, a piece of wood, a house; in a word, anything can be sacred. A rite can have this character. . . . There are words, expressions and formulae which can be pronounced only by the mouths of consecrated persons; there are sacred gestures and movements which almost anyone can perform. . . .

The circle of sacred objects cannot be determined then, once and for all. Its extent varies infinitely, according to the different religions.

(pp. 36-37)

Rudolph Otto (1869-1937)

The Idea of the Holy

AN INQUIRY INTO THE NON-RATIONAL FACTOR IN THE IDEA OF THE DIVINE AND ITS RELATION TO THE RATIONAL

By Rudolph Otto, translated by John W. Harvey, Oxford University Press (London: 1923).

Introductory comments by Tim Davis (2016).

> *Rudolf Otto was a German Lutheran theologian and philosopher who became one of the important and influential voices in early twentieth-century theology. In his work, The Idea of the Holy, he introduces the concept of the "numinous," which he believed was at the center of human religious experience throughout the world. Otto saw the encounter that humanity had with the "numinous" as both non-rational and non-sensory. It was a "feeling" that was outside of the self. He also believed the experience of the holy could manifest itself in two types of expressions which he terms "mysterium tremendum," the mystery that terrifies, and "mysterium fascinocium" (or "mysterium fascinans"), the mystery that attracts.*

Chapter II - NUMEN AND THE NUMINOUS (excerpts)

Holiness, or the holy, is a category of interpretation and valuation peculiar to the sphere of religion. It is, indeed, applied by transference to another sphere, that of Ethics, but it is not itself derived from this. While it is complex, it contains a quite specific element or moment, which sets it apart from the Rational in meaning . . . and which remains inexpressible or ineffable in the sense that it completely eludes apprehension in terms of concepts.

Chapter III - THE ANALYSIS OF MYSTERIUM (excerpts)

To keep a thing holy in the heart means to mark it off by a feeling of peculiar dread, not to be mistaken for any ordinary dread, that is, to appraise it by the category of the numinous. But the Old Testament throughout is rich in parallel expressions for this feeling. Specially noticeable is the *emah* of Yahweh (fear of God). . . .

Compare Exodus xxiii. 27: I will send my fear before thee and will destroy all the people to whom thou shalt come . . . ; also Job ix. 34; xiii. 21 (Let not his fear terrify me; Let not thy dread make me afraid). Here we have a terror fraught with an inward shuddering such as not even the most menacing and overpowering created thing can instill.

It will be felt at once that there is yet a further element which must be added, that, namely, of might, power, absolute overpoweringness. Thus, in contrast to the overpowering of which we are conscious as an object over against the self. There is the feeling of one's own abasement, of being but dust and ashes and nothingness. And this forms the numinous raw material for the feeling of religious humility.

This is already to be observed on the lowest and earliest level of the religion of primitive man, where the numinous consciousness is but an inchoate stirring of the feelings.

Representations of spirits and similar conceptions are rather one and all early modes of rationalizing a precedent experience, to which they are subsidiary. It lies rather we repeat, in a peculiar moment of consciousness, to wit, the stupor before something 'wholly other,' whether such an other be named 'spirit' or 'daemon' or 'deva,' or be left without any name. Nor does it make any difference in this respect whether, to interpret and preserve their apprehension of this other, men coin original imagery of their own or adapt imaginations drawn from the world of legend, the fabrications of fancy apart from and prior to any stirrings of daemonic dread.

Chapter VI - THE ELEMENT OF FASCINATION (excerpts)

The qualitative content of the numinous experience, to which the mysterious stands as "form" is in one of its aspects the element of daunting awefulness and majesty, which has already been dealt with in detail; but it is clear that it has at the same time another aspect, in which it shows itself as something uniquely attractive and fascinating.

These two qualities, the daunting and the fascinating, now combine in a strange harmony of contrasts, and the resultant dual character of the numinous consciousness, to which the entirereligious development bears witness, at any rate from the level of the daemonic dread onwards, isat once the strangest and most noteworthy phenomenon in the whole history of religion.

––––––––––––

Plainly, then, religion is only the offspring of history insofar as history on the one hand develops our disposition for knowing the holy, and on the other is itself repeatedly the manifestation of the holy. Natural religion, in contrast to historical, does not exist, and still less does innate religion.

––––––––––––

 It is not only in the religious feeling of longing that the moment of fascination is a living factor. It is already alive and present in the moment of solemnity, both in the gathered concentration and humble abasement of private devotion, when the mind is exalted to the holy, and in the common worship of the congregation, where this is practiced with earnestness and deep sincerity as, it is to be feared, is with us a thing rather desired than realized. It is this and nothing else that in the solemn moment can fill the soul so full and keep it so inexpressibly tranquil.

Karl Marx (1818-1883)

Critique of Hegel's Philosophy of Right

By Karl Marx, translated by Henry James Stenning in *Selected Essays*.
Introductory notes by Tim Davis (2016).

This excerpt is from Marx's famous essay on Hegel's philosophy where he both criticizes Hegel's idealism and decries religion as the "opium of the people". He wrote the introduction to the article in 1843 for the journal Deutsch–Französische Jahrbüche, which he was involved in publishing. The entirety of the reflection was not printed until a number of years later, shortly after Marx's death. The concept of religion worked its way into Marx's philosophy as a tool of the aristocracy, industrialists, and capitalists, which became a crutch of the underclass and working class. It was an illusory promise of hope in an afterlife that would be much better than their suffering in the present. Although it is likely that Marx saw religion as the way for the poor and downscast to cope, he also saw it as a form of protest (in a social justice sense) against their very suffering. He believed they should give up these illusions of "heavenly happiness" and demand the real earthly happiness that they deserved as human beings. Later interpretation of Marxist theory, particulalry by the Russian revolutionary Vladimir Lenin, saw religion as dragging down human advancement and retarding society. Based upon this idea, a number of Marxist–Leninist governments in the early twentieth century, such as the Soviet Union and the People's Republic of China, believed it beneficial to their cause to introduce state supported atheist policies.

The foundation of the criticism of religion is: man makes religion, religion does not make man. Religion indeed is man's self-consciousness and self-estimation while he has not found his feet in the universe. But man is no abstract being, squatting outside the world. Man is the world of men, the State, society. This State, this society produces religion, which is an inverted world-consciousness, because they are an inverted world. Religion is the general theory of this world, its encyclopædic compendium, its logic in popular form, its spiritualistic *Point d'honneur*, its enthusiasm, its moral sanction, its solemn complement, its general basis of consolation and justification. It is the fantastic realization of the human being, in as much as the human being possesses no true reality. The struggle against religion is therefore indirectly the struggle against that world whose spiritual aroma is religion.

Religious misery is in one mouth the expression of real misery, and in another is a protestation against real misery. Religion is the moan of the oppressed creature, the sentiment of a heartless world, as it is the spirit of spiritless conditions. It is the opium of the people.

The abolition of religion, as the illusory happiness of the people, is the demand for their real happiness. The demand to abandon the illusions about their condition is a demand to abandon a condition which requires illusions…

2

Native American Readings

Translations and transmissions by L. Spence (1908), G.B. Grinell (1913), G. Cronyn (1918), and T. Davis (2016)

Blackfeet

In Blackfoot mythology, the Old Man plays a very important role in a number of the creations stories. The Old Man can never die. A long time ago, he left the Blackfeet and disappeared into the mountains of the west. Before he departed, he told his people he would always watch over them and that someday he would return. Many who still believe in the old ways say that when he comes back he will bring with him many of the buffalo which have been hidden by the white men. Some say the Sun has now replaced the Old Man as the primary mythological figure.

Blackfoot Creation Myth,
as told to Dr. Tim Davis by a Blackfoot Elder

One of the most common legends tells that in the beginning the earth was covered entirely with water, but the Old Man was floating upon it on a huge raft accompanied by a number of animals. On a certain day the Old Man asked the beaver to dive into the water as deep as possible, go to the bottom, and bring up some mud. The beaver was under for a long time but finally returned to the surface, unsuccessful. Next he asked the loon to try, but the water was too deep and it also failed. The otter was next, but after great effort found the task too daunting. Finally the muskrat dove. He was gone for so long that the Old Man and animals gave him up for dead. It was only later that they spotted the near-lifeless body of the muskrat floating on the surface. They pulled him onto the raft and discovered in his paw a small bit of mud. The Old Man began to work with it and soon was able to fashion it into earth, the great lands and the mountains. After the land was formed, he then created humanity.

The Old Man and the Buffalo - Blackfoot Legend

(translation by G.B. Grinell, 1913)

The buffalo were essential to the Blackfeet. They lived in hunter-gatherer groups of less than 250 people. In winter they located near rivers in the valleys, but in the spring moved into the grasslands so they might benefit from the buffalo that

was so vital to their life and culture. Since they did not farm, the buffalo was
their major food source, in addition to fruits. They literally used every part of the
buffalo for their material existence and developed a close spiritual connection to
the animal as they believed that spirits had specially given them the buffalo for
the Blackfeet to survive.

At the Porcupine Mountains, the Old Man made earthen images of people, and blew breath on the images, and they came to life. They were men and women. After a time they asked him, "What are we to eat?" Then he took more earth and made many more images in the form of buffalo, and when he had blown on them they stood up, and he made signs to them and they started to run about. He then said to the people, "There is your food."

"Well now," they replied, "We have those animals, but how are we to kill them?"

"I will show you," he said.

He took them to the edge of a cliff and showed them how to heap up piles of stone. Coming back from the cliff where he created a narrow passage, he said to the people, "Now hide behind these piles of stones, and when I lead the buffalo this way, as they get opposite to you, stand up."

Then he went on toward a herd of buffalo and began to call them, and the buffalo started toward him and followed him toward the narrow passage until they were inside it. Then he ran to one side and hid, and as the people rose up, the buffalo ran on in a straight line and jumped over the edge of the cliff and some of them were killed by the fall.

"There," he said, "Go and take the flesh of those animals." Then the people tried to do so. They tried to tear the limbs apart, but they could not. They tried to bite pieces out of the bodies, but they could not do that. Old Man went to the edge of the cliff and broke some pieces of stone with sharp edges, and showed them how to cut the flesh with these. Of the buffalo that went over the cliff, some were not dead, but were hurt, so they could not run away. The people cut strips of green hide and tied stones in the middle, and with these hammers broke in the skulls of the buffalo and killed them.

When they had taken the skins from these animals, they set up poles and put the hides over them, and so made a shelter to sleep under.

IROQUOIS RITUAL OF FIRE AND DARKNESS

From *The Path on the Rainbow*, edited by George W. Cronyn, (1918), at sacred-texts.com

The members of the Ho-no-tci-no-ga Society assemble. Now the medicine doctor or shaman casts the sacred tobacco on the medicine-blaze, and in a low voice he chants:

Great Spirit who puts us to sleep in darkness,
We thank thee for the silences of darkness.
(Singer)
Now I ask blessing and make prayers.
(He sprinkles sacred tobacco on the fire.
Then he speaks to the Invisible.)
Now I give you tobacco,
You, the great Darkness!
(To the Thunder Spirit)
Now we act as we offer you tobacco!
You love it most of all offerings.
With it you will hear us better
And not tire of our talking
But love us with all power
Beyond all treasures
Or spreading of words through the air!
All men traveling under great heaven
You have invited, your grandchildren and all nations;
Oh you, maker of noise,
You, the great Thunderer!
Your grandchildren wish to thank you!
All your grandchildren have asked me
To offer this tobacco upon the mountain to you!
(Speaking to the Great Spirit)
You the All-maker,
Above-all-high
Best Friend of people!
We ask you to help us!
We implore your favor!
I have spoken.

pp. 6-7

PIMA RITUAL SONG CYCLE

THE FLOOD

From *The Path on the Rainbow*, edited by George W. Cronyn, (1918), at sacred-texts.com

I

ELDER BROTHER, SON OF EARTH

(Chanted by the People)

Dazzling power has Elder Brother,
Mastering the winds with song.
Swiftly now we come together,
Singing to gain control.

II

EARTH DOCTOR PROPHESIED THE FLOOD, CAUSED BY ELDER BROTHER:

Weep, my unfortunate people!
    All this you will see take place.
Weep, my unfortunate people!
    For the waters will overwhelm the land.
Weep, my unhappy relatives!
    You will learn all.
Weep, my unfortunate relatives!
    You will learn all.
The waters will overwhelm the mountains.

PIMA CREATION SONGS BY EARTH DOCTOR

from *The Path on the Rainbow*, edited by George W. Cronyn, (1918), at sacred-texts.com

Earth Magician shapes this world.
    Behold what he can do!
Round and smooth he molds it.
    Behold what he can do!

Earth Magician makes the mountains.
    Heed what he has to say!
He it is that makes the mesas.
    Heed what he has to say.
Earth Magician shapes this world;
    Earth Magician makes its mountains;
Makes all larger, larger, larger.

Into the earth the Magician glances;
    Into its mountains he may see.
I have made the Sun!
    I have made the Sun!
Hurling it high
    In the four directions.
To the East I threw it
    To run its appointed course.

I have made the Moon!
    I have made the Moon!
Hurling it high
    In the four directions.
To the East I threw it
    To run its appointed course.

I have made the Stars!
    I have made the Stars!
Above the earth I threw them.
    All things above I've made
And placed them to illumine.

pp. 86-87

THE HAKO: A PAWNEE CEREMONY

FIRST RITUAL

INVOKING THE POWERS

From *The Path on the Rainbow*, edited by George W. Cronyn, (1918), at sacred-texts.com

(EXPLANATION BY THE KÚRAHUS, OR CHIEF PRIEST)

At the creation of the world, it was arranged that there should be lesser powers. Tiráwa atius, the mighty power, could not come near man, could not be seen or felt by him, therefore lesser powers were permitted. They were to mediate between man and Tiráwa. The first song mentions some of these lesser powers in the order in which they come near to man, in the order of their creation.

INVOCATION TO THE GREAT SPIRITS

We heed as unto thee we call;
Oh, send to us thy potent aid!
Help us, Oh, holy place above!
We heed as unto thee we call.

We heed as unto thee we call;
Oh, send to us thy potent aid!
Help us, Hotoru, giver of breath!
We heed as unto thee we call.

We heed as unto thee we call;
Oh, send to us thy potent aid!
Help us, Shakuru, father of strength!
We heed as unto thee we call.

We heed as unto thee we call;
Oh, send to us thy potent aid!
Help us, h'Uraru, mother of all!
We heed as unto thee we call.

pp. 213-14

14

PRAYER TO THE MOUNTAIN SPIRIT

FROM THE NAVAJO

From *The Path on the Rainbow*, edited by George W. Cronyn, (1918), at sacred-texts.com

Lord of the Mountain,
Reared within the Mountain
Young Man, Chieftain,
Hear a young man's prayer!
Hear a prayer for cleanness.
Keeper of the strong rain,
Drumming on the mountain;
Lord of the small rain
That restores the earth in newness;
Keeper of the clean rain,
Hear a prayer for wholeness,
Young Man, Chieftain,
Hear a prayer for fleetness.
Keeper of the deer's way,
Reared among the eagles,
Clear my feet of laziness.
Keeper of the paths of men,
Hear a prayer for straightness.
Hear a prayer for courage.
Lord of the thin peaks,
Reared amid the thunders;
Keeper of the headlands
Holding up the harvest,
Keeper of the strong rocks
Hear a prayer for staunchness.
Young Man, Chieftain,
Spirit of the Mountain!

pp. 186-187

THE MAYAN *POPOL VUH*

Translation by Lewis Spence, Published by David Nutt, Sign of the Phoenix, Long Acre, London (1908)

There is no document of greater importance to the study of the pre-Columbian mythology of America than the Popol Vuh. It is the chief source of our knowledge of the mythology of the K'iche' people of Central America, and is of further considerable value when studied in conjunction with the mythology of the Nahuatlacâ Aztec Mexican peoples. This text comes from oral tradition performed in the sixteenth century and it is reputed to have been written down by a Christianized native of Guatemala sometime in the seventeenth century. In the early eighteenth century it was copied in the K'iche' language, in which it was originally written, by a friar of the Dominican Order of Preachers, one Francisco Ximenes, who also added a Spanish translation with scholia (marginal notes).

THE FIRST BOOK

Over a universe wrapped in the gloom of a dense and primeval night passed the god Hurakan, the mighty wind. He called out "earth," and the solid land appeared. The chief gods took counsel; they were Hurakan, Gucumatz, the serpent covered with green feathers, and Xpiyacoc and Xmucane, the mother and father gods. As the result of their deliberations, animals were created. But as yet, man was not. To supply the deficiency, the divine beings resolved to create manikins (human figures) carved out of wood. But these soon incurred the displeasure of the gods, who, irritated by their lack of reverence, resolved to destroy them. Then by the will of Hurakan, the Heart of Heaven, the waters were swollen, and a great flood came upon the manikins of wood. They were drowned and a thick resin fell from heaven. The bird Xecotcovach tore out their eyes; the bird Camulatz cut off their heads; the bird Cotzbalam devoured their flesh; the bird Tecumbalam broke their bones and sinews and ground them into powder. Because they had not thought on Hurakan, therefore the face of the earth grew dark, and a pouring rain commenced, raining by day and by night. Then all sorts of beings, great and small, gathered together to abuse the men to their faces. The very household utensils and animals jeered at them, their mill-stones, their plates, their cups, their dogs, their hens. Said the dogs and hens, "Very badly have you treated us, and you have bitten us. Now we bite you in turn." Said the mill-stones, "Very much were we tormented by you, and daily, daily, night and day. Now you shall feel our strength, and we will grind your flesh and make meal of your bodies." And the dogs upbraided the manikins because they had not been fed, and tore the unhappy images with their teeth. And the cups and dishes said, "Pain and

16

misery you gave us, smoking our tops and sides, cooking us over the fire, burning and hurting us as if we had no feeling. Now it is your turn, and you shall burn." Then ran the manikins hither and thither in despair. They climbed to the roofs of the houses, but the houses crumbled under their feet; they tried to mount to the tops of the trees, but the trees hurled them from them; they sought refuge in the caverns, but the caverns closed before them. Thus was accomplished the ruin of this race, destined to be overthrown. And it is said that their posterity are the little monkeys who live in the woods.

pp. 217-219

3

African Religion

Yoruba Legends

ORISA OKO

Translated by M. I. Ogumefu

ORISA OKO was a poor hunter, solitary save for his fife and his dog. If ever he lost his way out in the fields or the forest, he would begin to play some plaintive melody on his fife, and the sounds would lead the faithful dog to his side to guide him home.

He earned a meagre living by trapping in his nets guinea-fowls on the land of rich farmers, but because of his solitary life and his habit of silence, he was respected as a man possessed of secret knowledge which he did not care to divulge.

As years went by, he grew too old for hunting, and took up his residence in a cave. People now thought him more mysterious than ever, and came to him for advice about the future, so that in a short time he won great renown as a soothsayer. From far and near people came to consult him, and in this way he managed to live very comfortably.

In those days witchcraft was punished by death, and it became the custom in the country that anyone suspected of the evil art should be dragged to Orisa Oko's cave. If the soothsayer found him innocent, he led him forth by the hand, but if he were judged guilty, his head was cut off and thrown to the waiting crowd by the demon Polo, which Orisa Oko kept in the cave.

This went on until the old hunter's death. His followers now wished to continue the practice, and so they hid in the cave a very strong man to act as the demon Polo. When anyone accused of witchcraft was brought to the cave, his head was usually cut off and thrown out as before.

However, it once happened that a very tall and muscular man was suspected of magic arts, and his accusers succeeded in dragging him to the cave. A large crowd waited with eagerness to learn the result. What was their dismay to see

19

the head of the supposed "demon" Polo come rolling out of the cave, for the strong man had proved too much for him, and soon reappeared unharmed and triumphant.

The people were indignant to learn how they had been deceived, and from that day the cave of Orisa Oko was deserted.

pp. 12-14

THE IROKO TREE

In the forest there is a giant tree called by the Yorubas the "Iroko," which is shunned by all people, for in it lives the spirit of an old man who prowls about at night with a little torch and frightens travelers.

Anyone who sees the Iroko-man face to face goes mad and speedily dies.

Seeing the thick branches and mighty trunk of the Iroko, woodcutters are often tempted to cut the tree down and make use of the wood, but this is very unlucky, as it rouses the displeasure of the Iroko-man and brings misfortune on the woodcutter and all his family.

In any house which contains furniture made of Iroko-wood, there can be heard at night strange groaning and creaking noises; it is the spirit of the Iroko, imprisoned in the wood, who longs to wander about again through the forest with his little torch.

HOW TRIBAL MARKS CAME TO BE USED

A certain king named Sango sent two slaves to a distant country on an important mission.

In due course they returned, and he found that one slave had achieved successfully what he had been sent to do, while the other had accomplished nothing. The King therefore rewarded the first with high honors, and commanded the second to receive a hundred and twenty-two razor cuts all over his body.

This was a severe punishment, but when the scars healed, they gave to the slave a very remarkable appearance, which greatly took the fancy of the King's wives.

Sango therefore decided that cuts should in future be given, not as punishment, but as a sign of royalty, and he placed himself at once in the hands of the markers. However, he could only bear two cuts, and so from that day two cuts on the arm have been the sign of royalty, and various other cuts came to be the marks of different tribes.

Yoruba Religion

from *Yoruba-Speaking Peoples of the Slave Coast of West Africa*, by A. B. Ellis, (1894)

The priests, besides acting as intermediaries between the gods and men, preside at all trials by ordeal, and prepare and sell charms, amulets, &c. The priests of Ifa are diviners proper, but other priests also practise divination, though not with palm-nuts and the board peculiar to Ifa. The methods are various; one, called *keke*, is a casting of lots by means of small sticks or stalks of grass, each of which represents a particular individual; another, called *gogo*, is a drawing of lots. A certain number of grass stalks, one of which is bent, are held in the band or wrapped in a piece of cloth, so that the ends only show; and each person in turn draws one, the bent stalk indicating the one who is in fault. The person of a priest is sacred, and violence offered to one is severely punished.

The temples of tutelary deities of towns are usually to be found in the central square of the town, or near the principal gate, and those of the tutelary deities of families or households near the house-door or in the yard. In shape and construction they resemble the temples of the chief gods, but those of the protecting deities of households are mere miniatures, and are sometimes only small sheds, open at the ends and sides. Besides these structures, which are seen in every street, one often finds larger huts, circular in shape, thatched with grass, and large enough to contain a seated man. These, which might be mistaken for temples but for the fact that they contain no images, are built for the accommodation of pious persons who wish to meditate and pray. A temple is called *Ile Orisha*, "House of the Orisha."

Sacrifice is the most important part of ceremonial worship, and no god can be consulted without it, the value of the offering varying with the importance of the occasion. Besides the offerings thus made for special purposes, or on special occasions, persons who are the followers of a god-that is, those who wear his distinguishing badge and are believed to be under his protection-make, as a rule, daily offerings of small value, such as a few cowries, or a little maize-flour, palm-oil, or palm-wine.

Spirits of the Dead

from Yoruba-Speaking Peoples of the Slave Coast of West Africa, by A. B. Ellis, (1894)

The dead often return to earth, and are born again in the families to which they belonged in their former life. In fact, one might say that they always return, since every mother sends for a *babalawo* to tell her what ancestral ghost has animated her new-born child, and the *babalawo* always tells her which it is. As the births at least equal in number the deaths, and the process of being re-born is supposed to have gone on "from the beginning," logically there ought to be few, if any, departed souls in Deadland; but the natives do not critically examine such questions as this, and they imagine Deadland to be thickly populated, and at the same time every now-born child, or almost every one, to be a re-born ghost.

The soul, or ghost-man, after the death of the body, proceeds to Deadland, and food, drink, cowries (shells), and property of various kinds are placed in the grave with the corpse, to equip the ghost for his new sphere; while, before the grave is filled up, a goat is sacrificed to the deceased, and wishes offered for his safe journey, such as "May you arrive in peace," "May you not stray from the right path," etc.

The souls of the dead are sometimes reborn in animals, and occasionally, though but rarely, in plants. In the ideas of the natives, animals, though they differ in shape from a man, possess passions and moral qualities identical with those of the human being. Animals also possess souls which, like the souls of men, go to Deadland. Hence, as men and animals have so many characteristics in common, it does not require any great stretch of imagination for the native to fancy that the soul may be re-born in an animal.

The animal in which human souls are most commonly re-born is the hyena, whose half-human laugh may perhaps account for the belief. Human souls are also reborn in different kinds of monkeys, but chiefly in the solitary yellow monkey, called oloyo; and in these cases the human appearance and characteristics of monkeys no doubt furnishes the key to the belief.

Folk Tales of Nigeria

Why Dead People are Buried

Folk Stories from Southern Nigeria, by Elphinstone Dayrell, (1910), at sacred-texts.com

In the beginning of the world when the Creator had made men and women and the animals, they all lived together in the creation land. The Creator was a big chief, past all men, and being very kindhearted, was very sorry whenever any one died. So one day he sent for the dog, who was his head messenger, and told him to go out into the world and give his word to all people that for the future whenever any one died the body was to be placed in the compound, and wood ashes were to be thrown over it; that the dead body was to be left on the ground, and in twenty-four hours it would become alive again.

When the dog had travelled for half a day he began to get tired; so as he was near an old woman's house he looked in, and seeing a bone with some meat on it he made a meal off it, and then went to sleep, entirely forgetting the message which had been given him to deliver.

After a time, when the dog did not return, the Creator called for a sheep, and sent him out with the same message. But the sheep was a very foolish one, and being hungry, began eating the sweet grasses by the wayside. After a time, however, he remembered that he had a message to deliver, but forgot what it was exactly; so as he went about among the people he told them that the message the Creator had given him to tell the people, was that whenever any one died they should be buried underneath the ground.

A little time afterwards the dog remembered his message, so he ran into the town and told the people that they were to place wood ashes on the dead bodies and leave them in the compound, and that they would come to life again after twenty-four hours. But the people would not believe him, and said, "We have already received the word from the Creator by the sheep, that all dead bodies should be buried." In consequence of this the dead bodies are now always buried, and the dog is much disliked and not trusted as a messenger, as if he had not found the bone in the old woman's house and forgotten his message, the dead people might still be alive.

23

Why the Moon Waxes and Wanes

Folk Stories from Southern Nigeria, by Elphinstone Dayrell, (1910), at sacred-texts.com

There was once an old woman who was very poor, and lived in a small mud hut thatched with mats made from the leaves of the tombo palm in the bush. She was often very hungry, as there was no one to look after her.

In the olden days the moon used often to come down to the earth, although she lived most of the time in the sky. The moon was a fat woman with a skin of hide, and she was full of fat meat. She was quite round, and in the night used to give plenty of light. The moon was sorry for the poor starving old woman, so she came to her and said, "You may cut some of my meat away for your food." This the old woman did every evening, and the moon got smaller and smaller until you could scarcely see her at all. Of course this made her give very little light, and all the people began to grumble in consequence, and to ask why it was that the moon was getting so thin.

At last the people went to the old woman's house where there happened to be a little girl sleeping. She had been there for some little time, and had seen the moon come down every evening, and the old woman go out with her knife and carve her daily supply of meat out of the moon. As she was very frightened, she told the people all about it, so they determined to set a watch on the movements of the old woman.

That very night the moon came down as usual, and the old woman went out with her knife and basket to get her food; but before she could carve any meat all the people rushed out shouting, and the moon was so frightened that she went back again into the sky, and never came down again to the earth. The old woman was left to starve in the bush.

Ever since that time the moon has hidden herself most of the day, as she was so frightened, and she still gets very thin once a month, but later on she gets fat again, and when she is quite fat she gives plenty of light all the night; but this does not last very long, and she begins to get thinner and thinner, in the same way as she did when the old woman was carving her meat from her.

Rites of Passage to Manhood

Ikhom legend from a Nigerian village. Annotated by Tim Davis (2016)

In past days the young men of the Ikhom tribe were taken into the forest so that they could learn the secrets of true manhood and be initiated as adults into the life of the village. During this initiation period, the young men were sequestered and could have nothing at all to do with women. They were taken to a secret place in the forest, far away, where they performed the sacred tribal rituals.

One day, while the rites were being performed, a young girl who was simply walking through the sacred forest accidentally stumbled upon the group of young men in their camp. The initiates were right in the middle of one of their rituals so she hid in the bush, afraid of disturbing them and being discovered. The Ikom legend says, "But being a woman, she could not restrain herself from watching the secret rite." In fact, she continued to observe their activity through the day, all the while being undetected. As she watched, she could not help but notice a certain young man who she was continually drawn to.

When it was night, as the young men went to sleep, the young woman was so driven by attraction that she crawled into the camp and came up beside that certain handsome young man. Startled to see a woman at the sacred rites of passage, the young man quietly tried to persuade her to leave, fearfully reminding her that female presence was forbidden. The young woman impulsively began to profess her love for the young man and started to softly but passionately embrace him. The young man protested at first, but soon his objections turned to pleasure as he began returning her kisses. As their passion heightened, all of a sudden the young man stopped. His whole body began to shake. Immediately he began to stiffen, and then fell to the ground, dead. The young woman naturally cried out, and soon the other young men of the forest woke from their sleep. She tried to run away but the young initiates quickly caught up with her and took her back to the chief of the scared forest, the man who was in charge of the rituals. The chief then called upon the gods and asked if it was possible for the young man's life to be restored. It was not long before he received a message back.

The chief then returned to the village and called all the people together to hear the message from the gods. They were of course angry that the rites of the sacred forest had been violated, but he informed the people that in mercy the gods had told him how to save the life of the young man. "We are to construct a giant bonfire and are to throw a live lizard into the middle of it. If someone can run into the fire and save the lizard, the boy will be restored to life."

Soon the fire was prepared. The mother of the young man was the first to try, but the flames were too intense. His father followed but was choked by smoke and overcome by the intensity of the heat. The lizard was still alive, so the young woman, desperate to bring her loved one back to life, rushed into the middle of the blazing fire, and to the surprise of all the tribe, came out with the lizard. The young man immediately came back to life. But the people of the village decided that the violation of the sacred rites by the young woman was just too great. They pushed her back into the center of the fire that was at its height of intensity.

4

Hinduism

Rig Veda

Translated by Ralph T.H. Griffith, (1896), at sacred-texts.com
Re-edited and introduced by Tim Davis, (2016).

The Vedas, written down in Sanskrit between 1200 and 800 BCE, are the oldest surviving Hindu religious texts. Traditionally, Hindus believe them to be revelatory, authorless, not of human composition, but super-human. The term Veda, like the Jewish term Torah, can refer to specific early literature, but can also be viewed in a wider sense to encompass all of the tradition's scriptures. Here we are going to limit our use of the term Vedas specifically to the four earliest texts, namely: Rig Veda, Yajur Veda, Sama Veda, *and the* Athar-Veda. *Below we begin our selections with the older Rig-Veda. Each of these collections claim to represent a different approach to religious experience. The Rig-Veda are a collection of over one thousand flattering hymns of praise. The* Sama *were melodic songs. The* Yajur Vedas *were directed more toward ritual and sacrifice, and the later Atharva contain magical spells, incantations, and an expectation for the priesthood to facilitate extraordinary interventions between humans and the gods. Included below are just the first few verses of much longer Vedic hymns, to give the reader a feel for their tempo and intent.*

Book 2, Hymn 1, to Rudra (god of wind, storm, and the hunt)

1. What shall we sing to Rudra, strong, most bounteous, excellently wise,
   That shall be dearest to his heart?
2. That Aditi may grant the grace of Rudra to our folk, our cattle, and our progeny;
3. That Mitra and that Varuṇa, that Rudra may remember us,
   Yea, all the Gods with one accord.
4. To Rudra, Lord of sacrifice, of hymns and medicines,
   We pray for joy, and health, and strength.
5. He shines in splendor like the Sun, refulgent as bright gold is he,
   The good, the best among the Gods.
6. May he grant health into our steeds, wellbeing to our rams and ewes,
   To men, to women, and to the cattle.
7. O Soma (god of sacred elixir), set thou upon us the glory of a hundred men,
   The great renown of mighty chiefs.

Book 2, Hymn 2, to Agni

(god of fire, often invoked along with Indra and Soma)

1. With sacrifice exalt Agni who knows all life; worship him with oblation and a song of praise,
   Well kindled, nobly fed; heaven's Lord, Celestial Priest, who labors at the pole where deeds of might are done.

2. At night and morning, Agni, have they called to thee, like milk cows in their stalls lowing to meet their young.
   As messenger of heaven thou lightest all night long the families of men.
   Thou Lord of precious benefits and good events.

3. The Gods established him at the region's base, as doer of wondrous deeds, herald of heaven and earth;
   Agni the purely bright, like Mitra (the Sun deity) to be glorified among the folk.

4. Him have they set in his own dwelling, in the vault, like the Moon waxing, shining brightly in the realm of air.
   Bird of the sky, observant with his eyes, guard of the place as were, looking to Gods and men.

5. May he as Priest encompass all the sacrifice. Men come in throngs to him with offerings and with hymns of praise.
   Raging with jaws of gold among the growing plants, like heaven with all the stars, he quickens earth and sky.

Book 6, Hymn 18, to Indra

(A king of the Hindu gods in the Rig Veda, god of lightning, thunder, and rain. He is the destroyer of the evil dragon who brings drought to the land.)

1. Glorify him whose might is all-surpassing, Indra the much-invoked who fights uninjured.
   Magnify with these songs the never-vanquished, the Strong, the Bull of men, the Mighty Victor.

2. He, Champion, Hero, Warrior, Lord of battles, impetuous, loudly roaring, great destroyer,
   Who whirls the dust on high, alone, overthrower, hath made all races of mankind his subjects.

28

3. You, and you alone, have tamed the Dasyus (conquered and enslaved barbarian enemies); singly you have subdued the people for the Nobility. In this should your hero exploit, O Indra? Declare it at the proper season.

4. For truly, I deem, your strength is, yours the Mighty, yours O Most Potent, yours the Conquering Victor;
Strong, of the strong, Most Mighty, of all the mighty, thine, driver of the lowly and evil to acts of bounty.

Book 7, Hymn 75, to the Dawn

1. Born in the heavens the Dawn hath flushed, and showing her majesty comes as Law ordains.
She has uncovered fiends and hateful darkness; best of Aṅgirases (a noble patron family), hath waked the pathways.

2. Rouse us this day to high and happy fortune: to great felicity, O Dawn, promote us.
Vouchsafe us many and splendid riches, famed among mortals, man-befriending Goddess!

3. See, lovely Morning's everlasting splendors, bright with their varied colors, have approached us. Filling the region of mid-air, producing the rites of holy worship, they have mounted.

4. She yokes her chariot far away, and swiftly visits the lands where the Five Tribes are settled,
Looking upon the works and ways of mortals, Daughter of Heaven, the world's Imperial Lady.

Book 9, Hymn 2, to Soma

1. Soma, flow on, inviting Gods, speed to the purifying cloth:
Pass into Indra, as a Bull.

2. As mighty food speed hitherward, Indu, as a most splendid Steer:
Sit in thy place as one with strength.

3. The well-loved elixir was made to flow, the stream of the creative juice, the Sage drew waters to himself.

4. The mighty waters, yea, the floods accompanying the Mighty One,
When thou wilt clothe thee with the milk.

5. The lake is brightened in the floods. Soma, our Friend, the heavens prop and stay,
   The sacred juice falls on the purifying cloth.

6. The tawny Bull has bellowed, fair as mighty Mitra to behold:
   He shines together with the Sun.

Book 10, Hymn 175, to the Pressing stones of the Soma (sacred elixir)

1. May Savitar (minor solar diety) the God, O Stones, stir you according to the Law:
   Be harnessed to the shafts, and press.

2. Stones, drive calamity away, drive away malevolence:
   Make the sacred Cows our medicine.

3. Of one accord the upper Stones, giving the Bull his bull-like strength,
   Look down with pride on those below.

4. May Savitar the God, O Stones, stir you as Law commands for him
   Who sacrifices, pouring juice.

Sama Veda

Translated by Ralph T.H. Griffith (1896), at sacred-texts.com

Book III, Chapter I, Decade IV

To Indra

1. Pass by the wrathful offerer; speed the man who pours libation, drink
   The juice which he presents to thee!

2. What is the word addressed to him, God great and excellently wise?
   For this is what exalteth him.

3. His wealth who hath no store of kine hath ne'er found out recited laud,
   Nor song of praises that is sung.

4. Lord of each thing that giveth strength, Indra delighteth most in lauds,
   Borne by bay steeds, libations' friend.

5. With wealth to our libation come, be not thou angry with us, like
   A great man with a youthful bride.

6. When, Vasu, wilt thou love the laud? Now let the Channel bring the stream.
   The juice is ready to ferment.

7. After the Seasons. Indra, drink the Soma from the Brahman's gift:
   Thy friendship is invincible!

S. O Indra, lover of the song, we are the singers of thy praise.

Atharva Veda

Translated by Ralph T.H. Griffith (1896), at sacred-texts.com

Book 1 Hymn 12

A Prayer to Lightning, Against Fever, Headache, and Cough

1. Born from the womb, brought forth from wind and from the cloud, the first red bull comes onward thundering with the rain. Our bodies may he spare who, cleaving, goes straight on; he who, a single force, divides himself in three.

2. Bending to thee who clingest to each limb with heat, fain would we worship thee with offered sacrifice. Worship with sacrifice the bends and curves of thee who with a vigorous grasp hast seized on this one's limbs.

3. Do thou release this man from headache, free him from cough which has entered into all his limbs and joints. May he, the child of cloud, the offspring of the wind, the whizzing lighting, strike the mountains and the trees.

4. Well be it with my upper frame, well be it with my lower parts. With my four limbs let it be well. Let all my body be in health.

Laws of Manu

Translated by George Bühler in Sacred Books of the East (1886), Vol 25.
Re-edited and introduced by Tim Davis, (2016).

The Laws of Manu *are Sanskritic sacred texts, literally a collection of laws and guidelines, traditionally ascribed to Manu who was a sage and great teacher of ancient laws. Mythologically, Manu has also been seen by Hindu tradition as the first man or the son of the god, Brahma. Indian tradition says Manu was transformed into a king by Brahma to protect and lead the people and that he is responsible for the origins of kingship, institutions, and social classes. In ancient Hinduism, teachers of the various Vedic schools wrote manuals known as sutras in order to guide their students along the paths of their particular philosophies. The Laws of Manu is one such work. Written in meter, the oldest version of the Laws of Manu dates to around the second century BCE, but its transmission is likely several centuries older. The book deals with topics such as the creation of the world, sources of the dharma, the four early castes, the fruits of human action, moral choice, karma, rebirth, and moksha. Over the centuries various commentaries on the Laws of Manu have been compiled, the first know version of these possibly dates as early as seventh century CE. Modern translators have arranged the work into chapters. The following excerpts are abbreviated selections from much more detailed chapters in the Laws of Manu.*

Chapter 2

1. Learn that sacred law which is followed by men learned in the Veda and assented to in their hearts by the virtuous, who are ever exempt from hatred and inordinate affection.

2. To act solely from a desire for rewards is not laudable, yet an exemption from that desire is not to be found in this world: for on that desire is grounded the study of the Veda and the performance of the actions, prescribed by the Veda.

3. The desire for rewards, indeed, has its root in the conception that an act can yield them, and in consequence of that conception sacrifices are performed; vows and the laws prescribing restraints are all stated to be kept through the idea that they will bear fruit.

4. Not a single act here below appears ever to be done by a man free from desire; for whatever man does, it is the result of the impulse of desire.

5. He who persists in discharging these prescribed duties in the right manner, reaches the deathless state and even in this life obtains the fulfilment of all the desires that he may have conceived.

6. The whole Veda is the first source of the sacred law, next the tradition and the virtuous conduct of those who know the Veda further, also the customs of holy men, and finally self-satisfaction.

7. Whatever law has been ordained for any person by Manu, that has been fully declared in the Veda: for that sage was omniscient.

8. But a learned man after fully scrutinizing all this with the eye of knowledge, should, in accordance with the authority of the revealed texts, be intent on the performance of his duties.

9. For that man who obeys the law prescribed in the revealed texts and in the sacred tradition, gains fame in this world and after death unsurpassable bliss.

Chapter 10

1. Let the three castes discharging their prescribed duties, study the Veda. But among them, the Brahmins alone shall teach it, not the other two; that is an established rule.

2. The Brahmin must know the means of subsistence prescribed by law for all, instruct the others, and himself live according to the law.

3. On account of his pre-eminence, on account of the superiority of his origin, on account of his observance of particular restrictive rules, and on account of his particular sanctification, the Brahmin is the lord of all castes.

4. Brahmin, the Kshatriyan, and the Vaisya castes are the twice-born ones, but the fourth, the Sudra, has one birth only; there is no fifth caste.

5. In all castes those children only which are begotten in the direct order on wedded wives, equal in caste and married as virgins, are to be considered as belonging to the same caste as their fathers.

6. Sons, begotten by twice-born man on wives of the next lower castes, they declare to be similar to their fathers, but blamed on account of the fault inherent in their mothers.

7. Such is the eternal law concerning children born of wives one degree lower than their husbands. Know that the following rule is applicable to those born of women two or three degrees lower.

On the Vaisyas
Chapter 9

329. A Vaisya must know the respective value of gems, of pearls, of coral, of metals, of cloth made of thread, of perfumes, and of condiments.

330. He must be acquainted with the manner of sowing of seeds, and of the good and bad qualities of fields, and he must perfectly know all measures and weights.

331. Moreover, the excellence and defects of commodities, the advantages and disadvantages of different countries, the probable profit and loss on merchandise, and the means of properly rearing cattle.

332. He must be acquainted with the proper, wages of servants, with the various languages of men, with the manner of keeping goods, and the rules of purchase and sale.

333. Let him exert himself to the utmost in order to increase his property in a righteous manner, and let him zealously give food to all created beings.

On the Sudras
Chapter 9

334. To serve the Brahmins who are learned in the Vedas, householders, and famous for virtue is the highest duty of a Sudra, which leads to beatitude.

335. A Sudra who is pure, the servant of his betters, gentle in his speech, and free from pride, and always seeks a refuge with Brahmins, attains in his next life a higher caste.

336. The excellent law for the conduct of the four castes (varnas), when they are not in distress, has been thus promulgated; now hear in order their several duties in times of distress.

121. If a Sudra, unable to subsist by serving Brahmins seeks a livelihood, he may serve Kshatriyas, or he may also seek to maintain himself by attending on a wealthy Vaisya.

122. But let a Sudra serve Brahmins, either for the sake of heaven, or with a view to both this life and the next; for he who is called the servant of a Brahmana thereby gains all his ends.

123. The service of Brahmins alone is declared to be an excellent occupation for a Sudra; for whatever else besides this he may perform will bear him no fruit.

124. They must allot to him out of their own family a suitable maintenance, after considering his ability, his industry, and the number of those whom he is bound to support.

125. The remnants of their food must be given to him, as well as their old clothes, the refuse of their grain, and their old household furniture.

126. A Sudra cannot commit an offence, causing loss of caste, and he is not worthy to receive the sacraments; he has no right to fulfil the sacred law, there is no prohibition against his fulfilling certain portions of the law.

127. Sudras who are desirous to gain merit, and know their duty, commit no sin, but gain praise, if they imitate the practice of virtuous men (of higher castes) without reciting sacred texts.

128. The more a Sudra keeps himself free from envy and imitates the behavior of the virtuous, the more he gains. He does so without being censured or exalted in this world and the next.

129. No collection of wealth must be made by a Sudra, even though he be able to do so, for a Sudra who has acquired wealth, gives pain to Brahmins.

130. The duties of the four castes in times of distress have thus been declared, and if they perform them well, they will reach the most blessed state.

Upanishads

Translated by Friedrich Max Müller in *Sacred Books of the East* (1879), Vol 1.
Re-edited and introduced by Tim Davis, (2016.)

The Upanishads were written down in Sanskrit over the course of some two thousand years (through the period of the end of the Middle Ages). The majority were composed between 500 BCE and 200 CE but likely began earlier in an oral tradition. They are meant to be read in the form of an instruction, teaching, or dialogue between guru and student. The term Upanishad comes from the roots upasan or upa-na-shad which respectively mean to "draw near" or "sit down close to." Some see it as an instruction, or a sitting at the foot of the master. At the heart of these teachings is a process for investigating ultimate truth, in order that we might understand the nature of reality and that the soul might be allowed to become freed from our physical bodies. The Upanishads are traditionally considered to be a further unfolding of the ancient Vedas, so that these earliest teachings might continue to be meaningful for subsequent generations. Each Upanishad was composed in a certain place at a certain time for a certain purpose. Below is an excerpt from one of the earliest and most important of the Upanishads entitled, the Chandogya. It deals with ritual worship that is primarily connected to a meditation. These particular Chandogya Upanishads, possibly dating to the end of the sixth or first part of fifth century BCE, are often associated with the Sama Veda (written as a reaction to and "updating" of that literature).

There is a Spirit that is mind and life, light and truth and
vast spaces. He contains all works and desires and all perfumes
and all tastes. He enfolds the whole universe, and in silence is loving to all.
This is the Spirit that is in my heart. . . .

Chandogya Upanishad 3.14.2

My son, you cannot see the Spirit. But in truth he is here.
An invisible and subtle essence is the Spirit of the
whole universe. That is Reality. That is Truth. THOU ART
THAT.

Chandogya Upanishad 6.14

I am the whole universe.
Atman is above and below, North and South and East and
West. Atman is the whole universe.
He who sees, knows, and understands this, who finds in
Atman, the Spirit, his love and his pleasure and his union
and his joy, becomes a Master of himself. His freedom then is infinite.

Chandogya Upanishad 7.25

OM. In the center of the castle of Brahman, our own body,
there is a small shrine in the form of a lotus-flower, and
within can be found a small space. We should find who
dwells there, and we should want to know him.

Chandogya Upanishad 8.1.1

'The little space within the heart is as great as this vast
universe. The heavens and the earth are there, and the sun,
and the moon, and the stars; fire and lightning and winds are
there; and all that now is and all that is not: for the whole
universe is in Him and He dwells within our heart.'

Chandogya Upanishad 8.1.3

'There is a Spirit which is pure and which is beyond old
age and death; and beyond hunger and thirst and sorrow.
This is Atman, the Spirit in man. All the desires of this Spirit
are Truth. It is this Spirit that we must find and know: man
must find his own Soul. He who has found and knows his
Soul has found all the worlds, has achieved all his desires.'

Chandogya Upanishad 8.7.1

Chapter 14
Chandogya Upanishad

1. All is Brahman. Let a man meditate on that visible world as beginning, ending, and breathing in all that is the Brahman.

    Now man is a creature of will. According to what his will is in this world, so will he be when he has departed this life. Let him therefore have this will and belief.

2. The intelligent, whose body is spirit, whose form is light, whose thoughts are true, whose nature is like the air (omnipresent and invisible), from whom all works, all desires, all sweet odors and tastes proceed. He who embraces all this, who never speaks, is never surprised.

3. He is my self within the heart, smaller than a corn of rice, smaller than a corn of barley, smaller than a mustard seed, smaller than a canary seed or the kernel of a canary seed. The Brahman also is my self, within the heart, greater than the earth, greater than the sky, greater than heaven, greater than all these worlds.

4. He from whom all works, all desires, all sweet odors and tastes proceed, who embraces all this, who never speaks and who is never surprised, he, my self within the heart, is that Brahman. When I shall have departed from this world hence, I shall obtain him (that Self). For the spirit that is Brahman, is also my self. He who has this faith, has no doubt.

Bhagavad Gita

English translation by Swami Swarupananda (1909), at sacred-texts.com.
Introduction and comments by Tim Davis (2016).

*Just before a battle, the noble-born Arjuna, who is a commander, is questioning
the senseless killing of others, especially those who are his kin. He even believes
he will ultimately be punished for the taking of life. The god Krishna, who is
disguised as his chariot boy gives him a lesson in dharma (the code of conduct
required of him) and claims that being a good warrior and following the dharma
of his Kshatriyan caste is how he will attain reward in the next life.*

Chapter 1

Arjuna said:

29. Seeing, O Krishna, these my kinsmen gathered here, eager for fight, my
limbs fail me, and my mouth is parched up. I shiver all over, and my hair
stands on end. The bow Gândiva slips from my hand, and my skin burns.

30. Neither, O Keshava, can I stand upright. My mind is in a whirl. And I see
adverse omens.

31. Neither, O Krishna, do I see any good in killing these my own people in
battle. I desire neither victory nor empire, nor yet pleasure.

32-34. Of what avail is dominion to us, of what avail are pleasures and
even life, if these, O Govinda! for whose sake it is desired that empire,
enjoyment and pleasure should be ours, themselves stand here in battle,
having renounced life and wealth—Teachers, uncles, sons and also
grandfathers, maternal uncles, fathers-in-law, grandsons, brothers-in-law,
besides other kinsmen.

35. Even though these were to kill me, O slayer of Madhu, I could not wish
to kill them, not even for the sake of dominion over the three worlds, how
much less for the sake of the earth!

36. What pleasure indeed could be ours, O Jnanârdana, from killing these sons
of Dhritarâshtra? Sin only could take hold of us by the slaying of these
felons …

…………

45. Alas, we are involved in a great sin, in that we are prepared to slay our kinsmen, from greed of the pleasures of a kingdom!

46. Verily, if the sons of Dhritarâshtra, weapons in hand, were to slay me, unresisting and unarmed, in the battle, that would be better for me.

…….

Chapter 2

The Blessed Lord (Krishna) said:

2. In such a crisis, whence comes upon thee, O Arjuna, this dejection, un-Aryalike, disgraceful and contrary to the attainment of heaven?

3. Yield not to unmanliness, O son of Prithâ! Ill doth it become thee. Cast off this faint-heartedness and arise, O scorcher of thine enemies!

Arjuna said:

4. —But how can I, in battle, O slayer of Madhu, fight with arrows against Bhishma and Drona, who are rather worthy to be worshipped, O destroyer of foes!

5. Surely it would be better even to eat the bread of beggary in this life than to slay these great-souled masters. But if I kill them, even in this world, all my enjoyment of wealth and desires will be stained with blood.

6. And indeed I can scarcely tell which will be better, that we should conquer them, or that they should conquer us. The very sons of Dhritarâshtra,— after slaying whom we should not care to live,—stand facing us.

7. With my nature overpowered by weak commiseration, with a mind in confusion about duty, I supplicate Thee. Say decidedly what is good for me. I am Thy disciple. Instruct me who have taken refuge in Thee.

…………..

31. Looking at thine own Dharma, also, thou should not to waver, for there is nothing higher for a Kshatriya than a righteous war.

32. Fortunate certainly are the Kshatriyas, O son of Prithâ, who are called to fight in such a battle, that comes unsought as an open gate to heaven.

33. But if thou refusest to engage in this righteous warfare, then, forfeiting thine own Dharma and honour, thou shalt incur sin.

34. The world also will ever hold thee in reprobation. To the honoured, disrepute is surely worse than death.

35. The great chariot-warriors will believe that thou hast withdrawn from the battle through fear. And thou wilt be lightly esteemed by them who have thought much of thee.

36. Thine enemies also, cavilling at thy great prowess, will say of thee things that are not to be uttered. What could be more intolerable than this?

37. Dying thou gainest heaven; conquering thou enjoyest the earth. Therefore, O son of Kunti, arise, resolved to fight.

. . . .

Chapter 8

The Blessed Lord said:

3. The Imperishable is the Supreme Brahman. Its dwelling in each individual body is called Adhyâtma; the offering in sacrifice which causes the genesis and support of beings, is called Karma. . . .

5. And he, who at the time of death, meditating on Me alone, goes forth, leaving the body, attains My Being: there is no doubt about this.

6. Remembering whatever object, at the end, he leaves the body, that alone is reached by him, O son of Kunti, (because) of his constant thought of that object.

7. Therefore, at all times, constantly remember Me, and fight. With mind and intellect absorbed, in Me, thou shalt doubtless come to Me.

8. With the mind not moving towards anything else, made steadfast by the method of habitual meditation, and dwelling on the Supreme, Resplendent Purusha, O son of Prithâ, one goes to Him.

5

Buddhism

The *Dhammapada*

Introduction by Danya Furda (2016).

The Dhammapada, *or Dharma verses, is a collection of sayings in verse form attributed to the Buddha, Siddhartha Gautama, and is among the most popular of Buddhist scriptures (sutras) and a classic of religious literature. The* Dhammapada *consists of twenty-six chapters and is found in the Khuddaka Nikaya (minor collection), a subdivision of the Sutta Pitaka of the Pali Buddhist canon. These verses were circulated orally before being committed to writing around the third century BCE. A major theme of the* Dhammapada *contrasts the wise person with that of the fool and encourages its listeners/readers to follow wise advice on how to live a proper life. Below are a few sample verses from the first five chapters.*

Chapter 1 - The Twin Verses

The mind is the basis for everything.
Everything is created by my mind and is ruled by my mind.
When I speak or act with impure thoughts, distress follows me
As the wheel of the cart follows the hoof of the ox. (1:1)
The mind is the basis for everything.
Everything is created by my mind and is ruled by my mind.
When I speak or act with a clear awareness, happiness stays with me.
Like my own shadow, it is unshakeable. (1:2)
"I was wronged! I was hurt! I was defeated! I was robbed!"
If I cultivate such thoughts, I will not be free from hatred. (1:3)
"I was wronged! I was hurt! I was defeated! I was robbed!"
If I turn away from such thoughts, I may find peace. (1:4)
In this world, hatred has never been defeated by hatred.
Only loving kindness can overcome hatred.
This is an ancient and eternal law. (1:5)

Everything will end.
When I understand this, all quarrels fade away. (1:6)

As the wind topples a brittle tree
So will temptation topple me
If I am lazy, unrestrained, apathetic, seeking only endless pleasure. (1:7)
The wind cannot uproot a mountain.
Temptation cannot uproot me
If I am alert, self-controlled, devout, unmoved by pleasure and pain. (1:8)
When I see the truth as false,
When I believe illusion to be reality,
I am unable to find the truth. (1:11)

I must see the essential reality as real,
And discard illusion.
Only then can I find the truth. (1:12)

Chapter 2 – Mindfulness

Mindfulness leads to deathlessness
Carelessness leads to death.
When I am heedful, I need not fear death
But when I am negligent, it's like I am dead already. (2:1)
If a person is energetic and mindful,
Pure in deed, acting with consideration,
Self-controlled, and following the Truth,
Then he will be known and respected for his wisdom. (2:4)

When I am foolish, I live carelessly and become dull.
When I am wise, I cherish my awareness.
It is my most precious treasure. (2:5)
When my mindfulness drive away my spiritual slumber,
I climb the tower of wisdom, without attachment,
And view those trapped by their clinging.
Just as a person standing on a mountain gazes down at the world below,
I see without judgement those who suffer because of their delusions. (2:8)

Chapter 3 – The Mind

My mind is difficult to control.
Flighty and wild, it lands wherever it likes.
It is wonderful to control my mind,
Because a well-tamed mind brings happiness. (3:3)
My thoughts wander far and wide, traveling alone,
Bodiless and naked, sheltering in a cave within me.
When I master my thoughts,
I will be freed from the bonds of illusion. (3:5)
Enemies will hate each other,
Foes will harm each other.
But my own mind can harm me much worse. (3:10)
My mother, my father, my friends and relatives
Can love and assist me.
But my own mind can help me much more. (3:11)

Chapter 4 – The Flowers

My body is as impermanent as foam.
Its true nature is as a mirage.
Realizing this, I pluck out the flowers of illusion
And pass beyond death's sight. (4:3)
A bee collect pollen and then leaves, never harming the flower.
Neither the color nor the fragrance is diminished in any way.
In this way, I travel through life. (4:6)
Instead of focusing on the faults of others,
The wrongs they have done, the good they have failed to do,
I look clearly at my own acts,
What I do and what I leave undone. (4: 7)
Like a beautiful blossom with a rich, sweet scent
Are words of wisdom spoken by one who does not practice them. (4:8)
Like a beautiful blossom with a rich, sweet scent
Are the words of wisdom spoken by one who puts them into practice. (4:9)
Many different kinds of garlands can be made
With the same heap of flowers.
Many different kinds of good deeds
Can be done between my birth and death in this world. (4:10)
A heap of trash sits, discarded, by the side of the road

From out of it grows a beautiful and fragrant lotus flower. (4:15)
In the same way, out of the rubbish of this world,
A follower of the Buddha may grow,
With wisdom shining out among the blind. (4:16)

Chapter 5 – The Fool

A fool who knows he is a fool
Is wise, at least to that extent.
But a fool who believes himself to be wise
Truly fits the title "fool." (5:4)
Foolish people with poor understanding
Are their own worst enemies.
They plant the seeds of bad karma,
And when the plant grows to a tree, the fruit is bitter. (5:7)
When I do something but later regret it,
Weeping and mourning,
Then I should not have done it in the first place. (5:8)
But when I do something
And look back on it with true gladness,
Then it was a good deed to have done. (5:9)

Bloodstream Sermons

Introduction by Tim Davis (2016)

Buddhism had spread to China as early as the first century CE, but it was not until the Tang (唐) Dynasty (618-907 CE) that Buddhism reached the zenith of its popularity in China. Amid the flowering of other forms of Buddhism, the seventh century is when Zen (Chan) begins to grow. The story of the arrival of Chan (Zen) Buddhism in China often surrounds two figures: Bodhidharma (c. 440 – 528 CE) and the Chinese Emperor, Wu Ti (502-540 CE). Bodhidharma was a monk immersed in the Dhyannic Buddhist tradition in India. The Dhyannic masters of India were the precursors of Zen. They attempted to realize the Buddha nature through discipline of the body and mind in an effort to attain enlightenment. Their teaching did not necessarily have to rely upon written words or scriptures. They believed that to learn about the Buddha is to learn about oneself and to learn about oneself is to forget oneself. The Chinese Emperor Wu-Ti had extended lavish support to Buddhists in China, hoping to attain a good deal of "merit" for his efforts. His legendary encounter with Bodhidharma has been captured in a number of Buddhist legends. Some scholars have suggested Bodhidharma had already been living in China since the 470's, long before his legendary encounter with Wu Ti. A collection of texts attributed to Bodhidharma can be traced to the seventh and eighth centuries. The spontaneity and detachment for which they are known can be seen in the following excerpt.

Everything that appears in the three realms (earth, atmosphere, heaven) comes from the mind.
Hence Buddhas of the past and future teach mind to mind without bothering about definitions. . .
To search for enlightenment or nirvana beyond this mind is impossible. . . .
The Buddha is a product of your mind. . . .
To find a buddha you have to see your nature . . .
and a buddha is the person who is free . . . of karma, cause, and effect. . . .
Long ago, the monk, Good Star, was able to recite the entire Canon, but he didn't escape the wheel, because he didn't see his nature. . . .
Don't use a buddha to worship a buddha. . . .
The truth is, there is nothing to find. . . .

Huang-Po, Zen master (d.850)

When most people hear
That the Buddhas transmit the
Teaching of the One Mind,
They suppose that there
Is something to be attained
Or realized apart from mind,
And they use mind to seek the teaching,
Not realizing that mind and
The object of their search are one.
Mind can't be used to seek mind;
If it is, even after millions of eons
Have gone by, the search will still not be over.

Zen Koans

From *Zenrin Kushû*, compiled by Toyo Eicho (1429-1504). Introduction by Tim Davis (2016).

"Zen" is from the Sanskrit word "Dhyana," meaning "meditation." Zen Buddhism focuses on attaining enlightenment (bodhi) through meditation just as Siddhartha Gautama (the Buddha) did. In addition to meditation, the koans are stories that aid persons on the path to enlightenment. They are riddles that challenge rational and dualistic thinking. Meditating upon the answer to a koan allows one to come to peace with one's true self by going through a struggle which is designed to dissolve the rational mind and become a unified will of existence. There are over two thousand recorded koans. One riddle may take many years to solve. In Zen Buddhism, all humans have potential for enlightenment and for breaking the cycle of suffering and reincarnation, even in this lifetime. Zen rejects the study of scriptures, religious rites, devotional practices, and good works. The thirteenth century Japanese monk, Dogen Zenji, once said: "To study the Buddha Way is to study the self, to study the self is to forget the self, and to forget the self is to be enlightened by the ten thousand things." Some have suggested his style was meant to push the boundaries of logic and language, forcing the mind to abandon rational thinking. He maintained that a special kind of logic was needed to attain awakening. By examining all possible sides of a proposition or an idea, through exhaustive deconstruction one comes to a place of non-thinking. A number of these koans come from the Zenrin-Kushu collection of about five thousand koans compiled by Toyo Eicho, who was a student of Kanzan Egen (1277-1370) in the Japanese Rinzai school.

....

Sitting quietly doing nothing
Spring comes, and the grass grows by itself.

Zenrin Kushû

....

See the sun in the midst of the rain
Scoop clear water from the heart of the fire.

Zenrin Kushû

....

You cannot get it by taking thought;
You cannot seek it by not taking thought.

Zenrin Kushû

Like the sword that cuts, but cannot cut itself;
Like an eye that sees, but cannot see itself.

Zenrin Kushû

…………………………….

If you don't believe, just look at September, look at October!
The yellow leaves falling, falling, to fill both mountain and river.

Zenrin Kushû

………………………….

Fire does not wait for the sun to be hot,
Nor the wind for the moon to be cool.

Zenrin Kushû

……………………………..

We eat, excrete
Sleep and get up;
This is our world.
All we have to do after that -
Is to die

Ikkyû's Doka

…………………………..

A mind to search elsewhere
For the Buddha,
Is foolishness
In the very center of foolishness

Ikkyû's Doka

………………………………..

The flowers depart when we hate to lose them;
The weeds arrive while we hate to watch them grow.

Dogen Zengi

………………………………..

To be conscious of the original mind, the original nature -
Just this is the great disease of Zen !

Zenrin Kushu

………………………………..

Entering the forest he moves not the grass
Entering the water he makes not a ripple.

Zenrin Kushû

…………………………………

Two hands clapping makes a sound.
What is the sound of one hand clapping?

Hakuin

…………………………………

Jataka Tales

From *The Jataka*, Volume I, translated by Robert Chalmers, (1895), at sacred-texts.com. Introduction and minor editing of the translation by Tim Davis (2016).

> The Jataka *is a quite a large collection of Buddhist lore and fables framed as previous incarnations of the Buddha and Bodhisattvas who takes both human and animal form in the tales. They were originally written in the Pali language, the oldest in the collection dating to about 380 BCE. A number of them have traveled far and wide outside of the Buddhist world and often can be seen in parallel forms in western folklore and literature. In Theravada Buddhism the* Jataka *is considered part of Pali Canon. Some are even performed in theater and dance. The Theravada collection of stories numbers close to 550. Most other Buddhist traditions do not hold the* Jataka *in such high regard, treating them more as fables. Each tale usually has at its core some kind of moral. Many have theological or religious content. The following story seems to be an indictment of Hindu sacrificial practices and various attitudes held by the Brahmin caste.*

Matakabhatta Jataka 18

"If folk but knew."--This story was told by the Master while at Jetavana concerning Feasts for the Dead. For at this time the folk were putting to death goats, sheep, and other animals, and offering them up as what is called a Feast for the Dead, for the sake of their departed kinsmen. Finding them thus engaged, the Brethren asked the Master, saying, "Just now, sir, the folk are taking the lives of many living creatures and offering them up for the dead. Can it be, sir, that there is any good in this?"

"No, Brethren," replied the Master, "Not even when life is taken with the object of providing a Feast for the Dead, does any good arise therefrom. In bygone days, the wise, who had been reborn as Tree Fairies preached this Truth from mid-air, and showing the evil consequences of the practice, made the whole continent renounce it. But now, when the previous existences of the Devas had become lost to the people's minds, the practice had sprung up afresh." And, so saying, he told this story of the past:

Once upon a time when Brahmadatta was reigning in Benares, a brahmin, who was versed in the Three Vedas and world-famed as a teacher, sought to offer a Feast for the Dead. He had a goat fetched and said to his pupils, "My sons, take this goat down to the river and bathe it; then hang a garland round its neck, give it grain to eat, groom it a bit, and bring it back."

"Very good," said they, and down to the river they took the goat, where they bathed and groomed the creature and set it on the bank. The goat, becoming conscious of the deeds of its past lives, was overjoyed at the thought that on this very day it would be freed from all its misery, and laughed aloud like the smashing of a pot. Then at the thought that the brahmin who was about to slay him and thus bear the misery which the act would bear, the goat felt a great compassion for the brahmin, and wept with a loud voice. "Friend goat," said the young brahmins, "your voice has been loud both in laughter and in weeping; what made you laugh and what made you weep in that way?"

"Take me to your master and ask me your question before him."

So with the goat they came to their master and told him of the matter. After hearing their story, the master also asked the goat why it laughed and why it wept. Hereupon the animal, recalling its past deeds by its power of remembering its former existences, spoke thus to the brahmin: "In times past, brahmin, I, like you, was a brahmin versed in the mystic texts of the Vedas, and I, to offer a Feast for the Dead, killed a goat for my offering. By killing that single goat, I have had through a series of reincarnations, my head cut off five hundred times all but one. This is my five hundredth and last birth; and I laughed aloud when I thought that this very day I should be freed from my misery. On the other hand, I wept when I thought how, whilst I, who for killing a goat had been doomed to lose my head five hundred times, was to-day being freed from my misery, you, as a penalty for killing me, would be doomed to lose your head, like me, five hundred times. Thus it was out of compassion for you that I wept." "Fear not, goat," said the brahmin, "I will not kill you." "What is this you say, brahmin?" said the goat. "Whether you kill me or not, I cannot escape death to-day." "Fear not, goat" said the brahmin; "I will go about with you to guard you." "Weak is your protection brahmin", replied the goat, " and strong is the force of my evil-doing."

Setting the goat at liberty, the brahmin said to his disciples, "Let us not allow anyone to kill this goat;" and, accompanied by the young men, he followed the animal closely about. But the moment the goat was free of their sight, it reached out its neck to browse on the leaves of a bush growing near the top of a rock. And that very instant a thunderbolt struck the rock, rending off a sharp mass which hit the goat on the outstretched neck and tore off its head. And people came crowding round.

In those days the Bodhisattva had been born as a Tree-Fairy in that very same spot. By his supernatural powers, he was now seated cross-legged in mid-air while all the crowd looked on. Thinking to himself. 'If these creatures only knew the fruit of evil-doing, perhaps they would desist from killing,' in his sweet voice he taught them the Truth in this stanza:

If folk but knew the penalty would be

Birth unto sorrow, living things would cease

From taking life. Stern is the slayer's doom.

Thus, did the Great Being preach the Truth, scaring his hearers with the fear of hell; and the people, hearing him, were so terrified at the fear of hell that they left off taking life. And the Bodhisattva after establishing the multitude in the Commandments by preaching the Truth to them, passed away to fare according to his deserts. The people, too, remained steadfast in the teaching of the Bodhisattva and spent their lives in charity and other good works, so that in the end they thronged the City of the Devas.

6

Jainism

From *Jaina Sutras*, Part I, translated by Hermann Jacobi in Sacred Books of the East, Vol. 22, (1884).

ÂKÂRÂṄGA SÛTRA

FIRST BOOK

FIRST LECTURE

KNOWLEDGE OF THE WEAPON

FIRST LESSON

O long-lived (*Gambûsvâmin*)! I (Sudharman) have heard the following discourse from the venerable (Mahâvîra): (1)

Here many do not remember whether they have descended in an eastern direction (when they were born in this world), or in a southern, or in a western, or in a northern direction, or in the direction from above, or in the direction from below, or in a direction intermediate (between the cardinal points), or in a direction intermediate between these (and the cardinal points). (2) Similarly, some do not know whether their soul is born again and again, or not. Nor do they know what they were formerly, nor what they will become after having died and left this world. (3) Now this is what one should know, either by one's own knowledge or through the instruction of the highest (i.e. a Tîrthakara), or having heard it from others: that he descended in an eastern direction, or in any other direction (particularised above). Similarly, some know that their soul is born again and again, that it arrives in this or that direction, whatever direction that may be. (4) He believes in soul, believes in the world, believes in reward, believes in action (acknowledged to be our own doing in such judgments as these): 'I did it;' 'I shall cause another to do it;' 'I shall allow another to do it.' In the world, these are all the causes of sin, which must be comprehended and renounced. (5) A man that does not comprehend and renounce the causes of sin, descends in a cardinal or intermediate direction, wanders to all cardinal or intermediate directions, is born again and again in manifold births, experiences all painful feelings. (6) About this the Revered One has taught the truth (comprehension and renunciation). For the sake of the splendour, honour, and glory of this life, for the sake of birth, death, and final liberation, for the removal of pain, all these causes of sin are at work, which are to be comprehended and renounced in this world. He who, in the world, comprehends and renounces these causes of sin, is called a reward-knowing sage (muni). Thus, I say. (7)

pp. 1-3

SECOND LECTURE
CONQUEST OF THE WORLD
FIRST LESSON

Quality is the seat of the root, and the seat of the root is quality. He who longs for the qualities, is overcome by great pain, and he is careless. (For he thinks) I have to provide for a mother, for a father, for a sister, for a wife, for sons, for daughters, for a daughter-in-law, for my friends, for near and remote relations, for my acquaintances, for different kinds of property, profit, meals, and clothes. Longing for these objects, people are careless, suffer day and night, work in the right and the wrong time, desire wealth and treasures, commit injuries and violent acts, direct the mind, again and again, upon these injurious doings (described in the preceding lecture). (1) (Doing so), the life of some mortals (which by destiny would have been long) is shortened. For when with the deterioration of the perceptions of the ear, eye, organs of smelling, tasting, touching, a man becomes aware of the decline of life, they after a time produce dotage. Or his kinsmen with whom he lives together will, after a time, first grumble at him, and he will afterwards grumble at them. They cannot help thee or protect thee, nor canst thou help them or protect them. (2) He is not fit for hilarity, playing, pleasure, show. Therefore, ah! Proceeding to pilgrimage, and thinking that the present moment is favorable (for such intentions), he should be steadfast and not, even for an hour, carelessly conduct himself. His youth, his age, his life fade away.

A man who carelessly conducts himself; who killing, cutting, striking, destroying, chasing away, frightening (living beings) resolves to do what has not been done by any one. He and his relations with whom he lived together, will first cherish, and he will afterwards cherish them. But they cannot help thee or protect thee, nor canst thou help upon them or protect them. (3)

Or he heaps up treasures for the benefit of some spendthrifts, by pinching himself. Then, after a time, he falls in sickness; those with whom he lives together will first leave him, and he will afterwards leave them. They cannot help thee or protect thee, nor canst thou help them or protect them. (4)

Knowing pain and pleasure in all their variety, and seeing his life not yet decline, a wise man should know that to be the proper moment (for entering a religious life); while the perceptions of his ear, eye, organs of smelling, tasting, touching are not yet deteriorated, while all these perceptions are not yet deteriorated, man should prosecute the real end of his soul. Thus I say. (5)

pp. 15-17

FIRST BOOK

SEVENTH LECTURE

THIRD LESSON

Some are awakened as middle-aged men and exert themselves well, having, as clever men, heard and received the word of the learned. The noble ones have impartially preached the law. Those who are awakened, should not wish for pleasure, nor do harm, nor desire (any forbidden things). A person who is without desires and does no harm unto any living beings in the whole world, is called by me 'unfettered.' (1)

One free from passions understands perfectly the bright one, knowing birth in the upper and nether regions.

'Bodies increase through nourishment, they are frail in hardships.' See some whose organs are failing (give way to weakness).

A person who has no desires, cherishes pity. He who understands the doctrine of sin, is a mendicant who knows the time, the strength, the measure, the occasion, the conduct, the religious precept; he disowns all things not requisite for religious purposes, in time exerts himself, is under no obligations; he proceeds securely (on the road to final liberation) after having cut off both (love and hate) (2)

A householder approaching a mendicant whose limbs tremble for cold, may say:

O long-lived Sramana (ascetic)! Are you not subject to the influences of your senses?

O long-lived householder! I am not subject to the influences of my senses. But I cannot sustain the feeling of cold. Yet it does not become me to kindle or light a fire, that I may warm or heat myself; nor (to procure that comfort) through the order of others.

Perhaps after the mendicant has spoken thus, the other kindles or lights a fire that he may warm or heat himself. But the mendicant should well observe and understand this, that he may order him to show no such obsequiousness. Thus I say. (3)

pp. 66-67

Parable of the Man and the Well

This story is purported to have been told by a Jain monk to a prince in order that he might put into perspective the pitfalls of attachment to the physical world in which we all live.

From the *Samardicca Kaha* ii (55-8), adapted by Tim Davis (2016).

One day a man who had become despondent over his poverty and the miserable life he was living departed from his home in hopes of finding a better life in a land far away. He traveled through nearby towns, ports, villages, and cities but after a number of days, and much exhaustion, realized he was lost. He soon came upon a great forest that was closely packed with trees (and as he imagined, possibly full of wild animals). He entered the forest and began to find his way through its uncertain rough paths when just ahead there suddenly appeared a wild elephant that was not too pleased with encountering the man. He immediately began to charge at him, making frightening sounds and raising his trunk. But just as he began to turn and run, right before him instantly appeared a devil (of the feminine kind) who was brandishing a rather large and intimidating sword. She was hideous to look at and began to cry out in shrill and frightening tones. Fleeing in absolute terror he looked for some sort of refuge and just nearby noticed a large banyan tree which he thought might provide him with a means of escape. But by the time he reached the tree, his spirits were dashed, for its trunk was gigantic and slippery. There was no way for him to mount it. His whole body began to shake with fear as the elephant and demoness closed in. Preparing to die, craving for one more moment of existence, he happened to spot an old well near the foot of the tree. With reckless abandon he flung himself into it. Luckily the well was covered with grass and he was able to hold on to a clump of reeds that grew from inside its wall. The well appeared deep, and as the earth from which the grass grew began to crumble and give way, he began to hear the hiss of snakes below who were irritated by the droppings. As his eyes adjusted to the lack of light in the well, to his shock below, he saw a massive python that appeared to be as thick in diameter as the trunk of the elephant. He thought to himself, "My life will only last as long as these reeds can hold." Then, as if things could not possibly get worse, he looked up and noticed above him two large mice (one black, the other white), who with their sharp teeth were chewing at the clump of reeds which supported the man. By then the elephant had reached the well. Frustrated at not catching the man, he charged a number of times and butted the banyan tree which caused a beehive hanging from a branch above the well to shake free and fall upon our unfortunate victim. Immediately he began to be stung all over his body by a swarm of irritated insects. However, just as all appeared to be lost, by some chance a drop of honey from the hive had fallen upon his forehead, dripped down to his lips, and caused him the sensation of sweetness. He wanted more honey! Suddenly he thought nothing of the bees, the snakes, the mice, the elephant, or the demoness in his longing for more of the honey. In an instant he had forgotten the immediate perils of his life.

This story can be helpful to free the mind of those on the path to knowledge. Hear its meaning:

Now the man symbolizes the human soul as it exists in our physical body. It wanders through the forest of life. Th elephant symbolizes death (when it catches us), the demoness is our growing into old age. The banyan tree symbolizes salvation which is free of death, and yet no person with human senses can ascend it. The well symbolizes life, the snakes below are the passions that distract us. The python is the hell into which our suffering souls will fall upon. The reeds growing from the wall of the well are our lifetime. The mice, the nights and days we watch go by. The bees bring troubles, disease, and pain.

Those drops of honey are life's small pleasures. Why do we get so distracted by them, and desire them, amid a life that is filled with hardship, danger, and suffering?

7

Sikhism

Selections from the *Guru Granth Sahib*

Selections from the *Khalsa Consensus Translation* with much of the introduction from http://www.
sacred-texts.com/skh/index.htm

*The Granth is considered the living embodiment of the Gurus, the "eleventh
guru." Printed copies of the Granth are treated with the greatest respect. This is
the reason for the honorific titles that make up the full name of the book. There
are protocols to be observed while reading the Granth. A Sikh reader suggests
the following: "Out of respect, it is advised that before you do read the Sri Guru
Granth Sahib, that you cover your hair." This is normally with a turban or a
piece of cloth provided by the gurdwara (temple).*

*The Granth, compiled by Guru Gobind Singh (1666-1708), contains
compositions of six previous gurus, namely Guru Nanak, Guru Angad, Guru
Amar Das, Guru Ram Das, Guru Arjan, and Guru Teg Bahadur. The hymns are
arranged by the thirty-one ragas (musical forms) in which they were composed.
The hymns that comprise the Granth were originally written in several different
languages: Persian, mediaeval Prakrit, Hindi, Marathi, old Panjabi, Multani,
and several local dialects. In addition, there are Sanskrit and Arabic portions.*

Shri Guru Granth Sahib: Jup
Section 01 - Jup - Part 001

One Universal Creator God. The Name Is Truth. Creative Being Personified.
No Fear. No Hatred. Image of The Undying, Beyond Birth, Self-Existent. By
Guru's Grace -

Chant and Meditate:

True in The Primal Beginning. True Throughout the Ages.

True Here And Now. O Nanak, Forever and Ever True. ||1||

By thinking, He cannot be reduced to thought, even by thinking hundreds of
thousands of times.

By remaining silent, inner silence is not obtained, even by remaining lovingly absorbed deep within.

The hunger of the hungry is not appeased, even by piling up loads of worldly goods.

Hundreds of thousands of clever tricks, but not even one of them will go along with you in the end.

So how can you become truthful? And how can the veil of illusion be torn away?

O Nanak, it is written that you shall obey the Hukam of His Command, and walk in the Way of His Will. ||1||

By His Command, bodies are created; His Command cannot be described.

By His Command, souls come into being; by His Command, glory and greatness are obtained.

By His Command, some are high and some are low; by His Written Command, pain and pleasure are obtained.

Some, by His Command, are blessed and forgiven; others, by His Command, wander aimlessly forever.

Everyone is subject to His Command; no one is beyond His Command.

O Nanak, one who understands His Command, does not speak in ego. ||2||

Some sing of His Power-who has that Power?

Some sing of His Gifts, and know His Sign and Insignia.

Some sing of His Glorious Virtues, Greatness and Beauty.

Some sing of knowledge obtained of Him, through difficult philosophical studies.

Some sing that He fashions the body, and then again reduces it to dust.

Some sing that He takes life away, and then again restores it.

Some sing that He seems so very far away.

My mind is imbued with You, day and night and morning, O Lord; my tongue chants Your Name, and my mind meditates on You. ||2||

You are True, and I am absorbed into You; through the mystery of the Shabad, I shall ultimately become True as well.

Those who are imbued with the Naam day and night are pure, while those who die to be reborn are impure. ||3||

I do not see any other like the Lord; who else should I praise? No one is equal to Him.

Prays Nanak, I am the slave of His slaves; by Guru's Instruction, I know Him. ||4||5||

Sorat'h, First Mehl:

He is unknowable, infinite, unapproachable and imperceptible. He is not subject to death or karma.

His caste is casteless; He is unborn, self-illumined, and free of doubt and desire. ||1||

I am a sacrifice to the Truest of the True.

He has no form, no color and no features; through the True Word of the Shabad, He reveals Himself. ||Pause||

He has no mother, father, sons or relatives; He is free of sexual desire; He has no wife.

He has no ancestry; He is immaculate. He is infinite and endless; O Lord, Your Light is pervading all. ||2||

Deep within each and every heart, God is hidden; His Light is in each and every heart.

The heavy doors are opened by Guru's Instructions; one becomes fearless, in the trance of deep meditation. ||3||

The Lord created all beings, and placed death over the heads of all; all the world is under His Power.

Serving the True Guru, the treasure is obtained; living the Word of the Shabad, one is emancipated. ||4||

In the pure vessel, the True Name is contained; how few are those who practice true conduct.

The individual soul is united with the Supreme Soul; Nanak seeks Your Sanctuary, Lord. ||5||6||

Fifth Mehl, Gaat'haa
Section 37 - Fifth Mehl, Gaat'haa - Part 001

Associating with the Brahmin, one is saved, if his actions are perfect and God-like.

Those whose souls are imbued with the world - O Nanak, their lives are fruitless. ||65||

The mortal steals the wealth of others, and makes all sorts of problems; his preaching is only for his own livelihood.

His desire for this and that is not satisfied; his mind is caught in Maya, and he is acting like a pig. ||66||

Those who are intoxicated and absorbed in the Lord's Lotus Feet are saved from the terrifying world-ocean.

Countless sins are destroyed, O Nanak, in the Saadh Sangat, the Company of the Holy; there is no doubt about this. ||67|

One Universal Creator God
By The Grace Of The True Guru:

Camphor, flowers and perfume become contaminated, by coming into contact with the human body.

O Nanak, the ignorant one is proud of his foul-smelling marrow, blood and bones. ||1||

Even if the mortal could reduce himself to the size of an atom, and shoot through the ethers, worlds and realms in the blink of an eye, O Nanak, without the Holy Saint, he shall not be saved. ||2||

Know for sure that death will come; whatever is seen is false.

So chant the Kirtan of the Lord's Praises in the Saadh Sangat, the Company of the Holy; this alone shall go along with you in the end. ||3||

The consciousness wanders lost in Maya, attached to friends and relatives.

Vibrating and meditating on the Lord of the Universe in the Saadh Sangat, O Nanak, the eternal place of rest is found. ||4||

The lowly nim tree, growing near the sandalwood tree, becomes just like the sandalwood tree.

But the bamboo tree, also growing near it, does not pick up its fragrance; it is too tall and proud. ||5||

In this Gaat'haa, the Lord's Sermon is woven; listening to it, pride is crushed.

The five enemies are killed, O Nanak, by shooting the Arrow of the Lord. ||6||

The Words of the Holy are the path of peace. They are obtained by good karma.

The cycle of birth and death is ended, O Nanak, singing the Kirtan of the Lord's Praises. ||7||

When the leaves wither and fall, they cannot be attached to the branch again.

8

Chinese Religions

Daoism (Taoism)

Tao te Ching
Attributed to Lao Tzu

Translations and paraphrase by J. Legge (1891), L. Giles (1889). Re-edited by Tim Davis, (2016).

Chapter 1

The Dao that can be stated, is not the eternal Dao;
The name that can be named, is not the eternal name.
The nameless is the origin of the heaven and earth;
The named is the mother of ten thousand things.
So, by constantly having no desire, one views its wonders;
By constantly having desire, one views its limits.
These two have the same origin, but they differ in name;
Both are called Mystery.
One Mystery within Mystery, this is the source of all wonders.

Chapter 4

The Way is a limitless vessel;
Used by the self, it is not filled by the world;
It cannot be cut, knotted, dimmed or stilled;
Its depths are hidden, ubiquitous and eternal;
I don't know where it comes from;
It comes before nature.

Chapter 8

The best of man is like water,
Which benefits all things, and does not contend with them,
Which flows in places that others disdain,
Where it is in harmony with the Way.

So the sage
Lives within nature,
Thinks within the deep,
Gives within impartiality,
Speaks within trust,
Governs within order,
Crafts within ability,
Acts within opportunity.
He does not contend, and no one contends against him.

Chapter 14

They call it elusive, and say
That one looks, but it never appears.
They say that indeed it is rare,
One listens, but never a sound.
Subtle, they call it, and say
That one grasps it, yet never gets hold.
These three complaints amount
To only one, which is beyond all resolution.
By rising, it does not shine forth;
At setting, no darkness ensues;
It stretches far back to that nameless state
Which existed before the creation.
Describe it as form, yet unformed;
As shape that is still without shape;
Or say it is vagueness confused:
One meets it and it has no front;
One follows and there is no rear.
If you hold ever fast
To that most ancient Way,
You may govern today.
Call truly that knowledge of primal beginnings
The clue to the Way.

Chapter 22

Bend and be made straight
The rough places become smooth;
The pools shall be filled
And the worn renewed;
The needy shall receive
And the rich shall be perplexed.
So the Wise Man cherishes the One,
As a standard to the world:
Not displaying himself,
He is famous;
Not asserting himself,
He is distinguished;
Not boasting his powers,
He is effective;
Taking no pride in himself,
He is chief.
Because he is not a competitor,
No one in all the world
can compete with him.
The saying of the men of old
Is not in vain:
The crooked shall be made straight-
To be perfect, return to it.

Chapter 27

The skillful traveler leaves no traces of his wheels or footsteps;
The skillful speaker says nothing of which can be found fault or blamed
The skillful reckoner uses no tallies;
A good door needs no bolts or bars, but when shut is impossible to open;
The skillful binder uses no strings or knots, yet to un-loosen what he has
bound will be impossible.
In the same way the sage is always skillful at saving men, and thus he does
not cast away any man;
He is always skillful at saving things, and does not cast away anything.
Some call this 'Hiding the light of his procedure.'
Therefore, the man of skill is a master (to be looked up to) by him

who has not the skill; and he who has not the skill is the helper of (the reputation of) him who has the skill. If the one did not honor his master, and the other did not rejoice in his helper, an (observer), though intelligent, might greatly err about them. This is called 'The utmost degree of mystery.'

Chapter 32

The Way eternal has no name.
A block of wood un-tooled, though small,
May still excel the world.
And if the king and nobles could
Retain its potency for good,
Then everything would freely give
Allegiance to their rule.
The earth and sky would then conspire
To bring the sweet dew down;
And evenly it would be given
To folk without constraining power.
Creatures came to be with order's birth,
And once they had appeared,
Came also knowledge of repose,
And with that was security.
In this world,
Compare those of the Way
To torrents that flow
Into river and sea.

Chapter 40

Scholars of the highest class, when they hear about the Tao, earnestly carry it into practice. Scholars of the middle class, when they have heard about it, seem now to keep it and now to lose it. Scholars of the lowest class, when they have heard about it, laugh greatly at it. If it were not (thus) laughed at, it would not be fit to be the Tao,
Therefore, the sentence-makers have thus expressed themselves:
'The Tao, when brightest seen, seems to have light to lack;

Those who progress in it make, seem to keep drawing back;
Its even way is like a rugged track.
Its highest virtue from the valley does rise;
Its greatest beauty seems to offend the eyes;
And yet, he has most whose lot in life is least supplied.
Its firmest virtue seems but poor and low;
Its solid truth seems change to go;
Its largest square does no corner show.
A vessel great, it is the slowest made;
Loud is its sound, but never a word it said;
A semblance great, the shadow of a shade.
The Tao is hidden, and has no name; but it is the Tao which is
skillful at imparting to all things what they need and making them complete.'

Chapter 78

Nothing is weaker than water,
But when it attacks something hard
Or resistant, then nothing withstands it,
And nothing will alter its way.
Everyone knows this, that weakness prevails
Over strength and that gentleness conquers
The adamant hindrance of men, but that
 Nobody demonstrates how it is so.
Because of this the Wise Man says
That only one who bears the nations shame
Is fit to be its hallowed lord;
That only one who takes upon himself
 The evils of the world may be its king.
This is the paradox.

Public Domain works:

Tao te Ching by Lao Tzu, Translated by J. Legge, in *Sacred Books of the East*, Vol 39, 1891

The Sayings of Lao Tzu by Lionel Giles in the Wisdom of the Earth Series, (New York) E.P. Dutton, 1905.

Chuang Tzu

Translations and paraphrase by H. Giles (1889) and Tim Davis (2016)

*Also known as **Zhuang Zhou** or **Zhuangzi**, Chuang Tzu (369-286 BCE) lived during the period of the Warring States. He is traditionally credited by scholars with at least part of the work which bears his name. The stories, allegories, poems and philosophies that make up the work are reflective of the carefree Taoist existence Chuang Tzu exemplified. Often humorous, simple, but deeply penetrating, his anecdotes attempt to demonstrate humanity's misunderstanding of life's distinctions between good and evil, grand and small, life and death, humanity and nature. The sole account of his life comes from some brief comments in chapter 63 of Sima Qian's* Records of the Grand Historian *but are most likely primarily gleaned from the work Chuang Tzu.*

Chuang Tzu and his followers perceived a naturally shifting universe which operated without the intervention of gods or some divine plan steering it. Humans live in relationship within a world where the goal is happiness and we achieve this by spontaneously living in the moment. The trap we fall into is forgetting what is natural by creating artificial constructions or distinctions which cloud our mind of true reality.

During the time of Chuang Tzu, Taoism exerted much less societal influence than Confucianism. To correctly put Chuang Tzu's work into perspective, we should then look at it against the backdrop of a culture that was strongly and positively affected by Confucian teachings which were often rooted in ideologies that he himself was quite often eager to criticize. His disagreements and philosophical differences also extended to other schools of Chinese thought such as that of Mo Ti (470-391 BCE), the Legalists, and even his contemporary friend (and frequent adversary), the logician, Hui Tzu. (See a brief example of this in the "Joy of the Fishes" excerpt which follows).

We should also see Chuang Tzu in relation to the events that followed him. He was not part of the popular superstitions, magic, alchemy, and health-centered culture which occurred in Taoist China during later periods. Those who benefited most from his works are the Chinese Zen Buddhists of the Tang period (seventh to tenth centuries CE.). However, as one of the great writers of the classical Chinese period, Chuang Tzu's work continued to influence Chinese thought in a variety of ways throughout China's entire history.

The Great Supreme

For Tao has its inner reality and its evidences.
It is devoid of action and of form.
It may be transmitted, but cannot be received;
It may be obtained, but cannot be seen.
It is based in itself, rooted in itself.
Before heaven and earth were,
Tao existed by itself from all time.
It gave the spirits and rulers their spiritual powers,
and gave Heaven and Earth their birth.
To Tao, the zenith is not high,
nor the nadir low;
no point in time is long ago,
nor by the lapse of ages has it grown old.

On Leveling All Things

Whether the soul is locked in sleep
or whether in waking hours the body moves,
we are striving and struggling with the immediate circumstances.
Some are easy-going and leisurely,
some are deep and cunning,
and some are secretive.
Now we are frightened over petty fears,
now disheartened and dismayed over some great terror.
Now the mind flies forth like an arrow from a cross-bow,
to be the arbiter of right and wrong.
Now it stays behind as if sworn to an oath,
 to hold on to what it has secured.
Then, as under autumn and winter's blight,
comes gradual decay,
and submerged in its own occupations,
it keeps on running its course,
never to return.
Finally, worn out and imprisoned,
it is choked up like an old drain,
and the failing mind shall not see light again.

Opening Trunks, A Protest Against Civilization

There is often chaos in the world,
and the love of knowledge is ever at the bottom of it.
For all men strive to grasp what they do not know,
while none strive to grasp what they already know;
and all strive to discredit what they do not excel in,
while none strive to discredit what they do excel in.
That is why there is chaos.
Thus, above, the splendor of the heavenly bodies is dimmed;
below, the power of land and water is burned up,
while in between the influence of the four seasons is upset.
There is not one tiny worm that moves on earth
or insect that flies in the air
but has lost its original nature.
Such indeed is the world chaos caused by the desire for knowledge!
Ever since the time of the Three Dynasties downwards,
it has been like this.
The simple and the guileless have been set aside;
the specious and the cunning have been exalted.
Tranquil inaction has given place to love of disputation;
and disputation alone is enough to bring chaos upon the world.

Chuang Tzu's Butterfly Dream

Once upon a time, I, Chuang Tzu , dreamt I was a butterfly, fluttering hither
and thither, to all intents and purposes a butterfly. I was conscious only of my
happiness as a butterfly, unaware that I was Chou. Soon I awaked, and there
I was, veritably myself again. Now I do not know whether I was then a man
dreaming I was a butterfly, or whether I am now a butterfly, dreaming I am
a man. Between a man and a butterfly there is necessarily a distinction. The
transition is called the transformation of material things.

The Identity of Contraries

Tao which shines forth is not Tao.
Speech which argues falls short of its aim.
Charity which has fixed points loses its scope.

Honesty which is absolute is wanting in credit.
 Courage which is absolute misses its object.
These five are, as it were, round, with a strong bias towards squareness.
Therefore that knowledge which stops
 at what it does not know, is the highest knowledge.
Who knows the argument which can be argued without words?
The Tao which does not declare itself as Tao?
 He who knows this may be said to be of God.
To be able to pour in without making full,
 And pour out without making empty,
In ignorance of the power
By which such results are accomplished —

(pp. 25-26 of Giles)

Born in Tao

Fishes are born in water.
Man is born in the Tao.
If fishes get ponds to live in,
they thrive.
If man gets Tao to live in,
he may live his life in peace.
Without reference to the outward ceremonial of this world.
Hence the saying, 'All that a fish wants is water;
all that a man wants is Tao.'

(p. 28 of Giles)

The Joy of the Fishes

Chuang Tzu and Hui Tzu were crossing a bridge at the dam on the Hao river

"The small fish dart and leap so happily and freely," said Chuang,

"They surely must be in a state of happiness."

75

But Hui responded: "It seems that if you are not a fish, how can you know their happiness?"

Chuang then said: "Well then, because you are not a fish, how can you then know that I am not aware of what makes these fish happy?"

Hui then argued: "If I, not being you, am unable to know exactly what is in your mind, it must follow that you, who are not a fish, cannot know what these fish are experiencing."

Chuang paused and then replied: "Now wait, let's go back to your original comment. You asked how can I know what makes the fish happy. It seems that from the terms of your question might know that I do know what makes fishes happy.

"I know the joy of fish in the river because of my own joy, as I go walking along the very same river."

Evidence of a Full Character

A man does not seek to see himself in running water, but in still water.

For only what is itself still can instill stillness into others.

The grace of earth has reached only the pines and cedars; winter and summer alike, they are green.

The grace of God has reached to Yao and to Shun, who alone attained rectitude.

Happily he was able to rectify himself and thus become the means through which all were rectified.

For the possession of one's original nature is evidenced in true courage.

Public Domain Works:

Chuang Tzu in *Wisdom of China* from *Chuangtse, Mystic and Humorist*, http://scrye.com/~station /ChuangTzu.html

Chuang Tzu: Mystic, Moralist, and Social Reformer by Herbert A. Giles, London: Bernard Quaritch, 1889.

Confucianism

The Analects

Translated by James Legge in *The Chinese Classics* (1893)

Book IV Le Jin

CHAP. VIII. The Master said, 'If a man in the morning hear the right way, he may die in the evening without regret."

CHAP. IX. The Master said, 'A scholar, whose mind is set on truth, and who is ashamed of bad clothes and bad food, is not fit to be discoursed with.'

CHAP. X. The Master said, 'The superior man, in the world, does not set his mind either for anything, or against anything; what is right he will follow.'

CHAP. XI. The Master said, 'The superior man thinks of virtue; the small man thinks of comfort. The superior man thinks of the sanctions of law; the small man thinks of favors which he may receive.'

Book VI Yung Yey

CHAP. XVIII. The Master said, 'They who know the truth are not equal to those who love it, and they who love it are not equal to those who delight in it.'

CHAP. XIX. The Master said, 'To those whose talents are above mediocrity, the highest subjects may be announced. To those who are below mediocrity, the highest subjects may not be announced.'

CHAP. XX. Fan Ch'ih asked what constituted wisdom. The Master said, 'To give one's self earnestly to the duties due to men, and, while respecting spiritual beings, to keep aloof from them, may be called wisdom.' He asked about perfect virtue. The Master said, 'The man of virtue makes the difficulty to be overcome his first business, and success only a subsequent consideration; this may be called perfect virtue.'

Book VIII T'Ai-Po

CHAP. IV. 1. The philosopher Tsang being ill, Meng Chang went to ask how he was.

2. Tsang said to him, 'When a bird is about to die, its notes are mournful; when a man is about to die, his words are good.

3. 'There are three principles of conduct which the man of high rank should consider specially important:--that in his deportment and manner he keep from violence and heedlessness; that in regulating his countenance he keep near to sincerity; and that in his words and tones he keep far from lowness and impropriety. As to such matters as attending to the sacrificial vessels, there are the proper officers for them.'

Book XII Yen Yuan

CHAP. II. Chung-kung asked about perfect virtue. The Master said, 'It is, when you go abroad, to behave to every one as if you were receiving a great guest; to employ the people as if you were assisting at a great sacrifice; not to do to others as you would not wish done to yourself; to have no murmuring against you in the country, and none in the family.' Chung-kung said, 'Though I am deficient in intelligence and vigor, I will make it my business to practice this lesson.'

CHAP. III. 1. Sze-ma Niu asked about perfect virtue.

2. The Master said, 'The man of perfect virtue is cautious and slow in his speech.'

Book XV Wei Ling Kung

CHAP. XVII. The Master said, 'The superior man in everything considers righteousness to be essential. He performs it according to the rules of propriety. He brings it forth in humility. He completes it with sincerity. This is indeed a superior man.'

CHAP. XVIII. The Master said, 'The superior man is distressed by his want of ability. He is not distressed by men's not knowing him.'

CHAP. XIX. The Master said, 'The superior man dislikes the thought of his name not being mentioned after his death.'

CHAP. XX. The Master said, 'What the superior man seeks, is in himself. What the mean man seeks, is in others.'

CHAP. XXI. The Master said, 'The superior man is dignified, but does not wrangle. He is sociable, but not a partisan.'

CHAP. XXII. The Master said, 'The superior man does not promote a man simply on account of his words, nor does he put aside good words because of the man.'

CHAP. XXIII. Tsze-kung asked, saying, 'Is there one word which may serve as a rule of practice for all one's life?' The Master said, 'Is not RECIPROCITY such a word? What you do not want done to yourself, do not do to others.'

CHAP. XXIV. 1. The Master said, 'In my dealings with men, whose evil do I blame, whose goodness do I praise, beyond what is proper? If I do sometimes exceed in praise, there must be ground for it in my examination of the individual.

2. 'This people supplied the ground why the three dynasties pursued the path of straightforwardness.'

CHAP. XXV. The Master said, 'Even in my early days, a historiographer would leave a blank in his text, and he who had a horse would lend him to another to ride. Now, alas! there are no such things.'

Book XVI Ke She

CHAP. X. Confucius said, 'The superior man has nine things which are subjects with him of thoughtful consideration. In regard to the use of his eyes, he is anxious to see clearly. Inregard to the use of his ears, he is anxious to hear distinctly. In regard to his countenance, he is anxious that it should be benign. In regard to his demeanor, he is anxious that it should be respectful. In regard to his speech, he is anxious that it should be sincere. In regard to his doing of business, he is anxious that it should be reverently careful. In regard to what he doubts about, he is anxious to question others. When he is angry, he thinks of the difficulties (his anger may involve him in). When he sees gain to be got, he thinks of righteousness.'

CHAP. XI. 1. Confucius said, 'Contemplating good, and pursuing it, as if they could not reach it; contemplating evil, and shrinking from it, as they would from thrusting the hand into boiling water.'

Li Ki (The Book of Rites)

Translated by James Legge (1885) in *Sacred Books of the East*, Vol. 27

Book I

Ch. 1. 1. The Summary of the Rules of Propriety says: Always and in everything let there be reverence; with deportment, seriousness, as when one is thinking (deeply), and with speech be composed and definite. This will make the people tranquil.

2. Pride should not be allowed to grow; the desires should not be indulged; the will should not be gratified to the full; pleasure should not be carried to excess.

3. Men of talents and virtue can be familiar with others and yet respect them; can stand in awe of others and yet love them. They love others and yet acknowledge the evil that is in them. They accumulate (wealth) and yet are able to part with it (to help the needy); they rest in what gives them satisfaction and yet can seek satisfaction elsewhere (when it is desirable to do so). 4. When you find wealth within your reach, do not (try to) get it by improper means; when you meet with calamity, do not (try to) escape from it by improper means. Do not seek for victory in small contentions; do not seek for more than your proper share. 5. Do not positively affirm what you have doubts about; and (when you have no doubts), do not let what you say appear (simply) as your own view[1].

Book II

6. When Confucius had succeeded in burying (his mother) in the same grave (with his father) at Fang, he said, 'I have heard that the ancients made graves (only), and raised no mound over them. But I am a man, who will be (travelling) east, west, south, and north. I cannot do without something by which I can remember (the place).' On this, he (resolved to) raise a mound (over the grave) four feet high. He then first returned, leaving the disciples behind. A great rain came on; and when they rejoined him, he asked them

what had made them so late. 'The earth slipped,' they said, 'from the grave at Fang.' They told him this thrice without his giving them any answer. He then wept freely, and said, 'I have heard that the ancients did not need to repair their graves.'

Book III

5. Where any of the spirits of the hills and rivers had been unattended to, it was held to be an act of irreverence, and the irreverent ruler was deprived of a part of his territory. Where there had been neglect of the proper order in the observances of the ancestral temple, it was held to show a want of filial piety and the rank of the unfilial ruler was reduced. Where any ceremony had been altered, or any instrument of music changed, it was held to be an instance of disobedience, and the disobedient ruler was banished. Where the statutory measures and the (fashion of) clothes had been changed, it was held to be rebellion, and the rebellious ruler was taken off. The ruler who had done good service for the people, and shown them an example of virtue, received an addition to his territory and rank.

Book VI

4. That the descendants of the five rulers, to whom the temple-shrines were dedicated, were required, so long as the shrine of the grand ancestor had not been removed, to announce their cappings (male rite of passage to adulthood) and marriages, and their death was also required to be announced, showed how kinship was to be kept in mind [2]. While the kinship was yet maintained, that some were classed among the common people showed how mean (middle) position followed on want of ability. The reverent observance of condoling, wailing, and of presenting contributions to the funeral rites in articles and money was the way taken to maintain harmony and tradition. The ancient kings made use of the stalks and the tortoise-shell; arranged their sacrifices; buried their offerings of silk; recited their words of supplication and benediction; and made their statutes and measures. In this way arose the ceremonial usages of the states, the official departments with their administrators, each separate business with its own duties, and the rules of ceremony in their orderly arrangements.

Book VI Section IV

2. Thus it was that the ancient kings were troubled lest the ceremonial usages should not be generally understood by all below them. They therefore

sacrificed to God in the suburb (of the capital), and thus the place of heaven was established. They sacrificed at the altar of the earth inside the capital, and thus they intimated the benefits derived from the earth. Their sacrifices in the ancestral temple gave their fundamental place to the sentiments of humanity. Those at the altars of the hills and streams served to mark their intercourse with the spirits breathing (in nature). Their five sacrifices (of the house) were a recognition of the various business which was to be done.

For the same reason, there are the officers of prayer in the ancestral temple; the three ministers of the dukes in the court; and the three classes of old men in the college. In front of the king there were the sorcerers, and behind him the recorders; the diviners by the tortoise-shell and by the stalks, the blind musicians and their helpers were all on his left and right. He himself was in the center. His mind had nothing to do but to maintain what was entirely correct.

3. By means of the ceremonies performed in the suburb, all the spirits receive their offices. By means of those performed at the altar of the earth, all the things yielded (by the earth) receive their fullest development. By means of those in the ancestral temple, the services of filial duty and of kindly affection come to be discharged. By means of those at the five sacrifices of the house, the laws and rules of life are correctly exhibited. Hence when the ideas in these sacrifices in the suburb, at the altar of the earth, in the ancestral temple, at the altars of the hills and streams, and of the five sacrifices of the house are fully apprehended, the ceremonies used are found to be lodged in them[1].

9

Shinto

THE *YENGISHIKI* OR SHINTO RITUALS

INTERNET SACRED TEXT ARCHIVE http://www.sacred-texts.com/shi/yengi.htm (Public Domain)

THE FIRE RITUAL

I declare with the great ritual, the Heavenly ritual, which was bestowed on him at the time when, by the Word of the Sovereign's dear progenitor and progenitrix, who divinely remain in the plain of high Heaven, they bestowed on him the region under Heaven, saying: "Let the Sovereign Grandchild's augustness tranquilly rule over the country of fresh spikes which flourishes in the midst of the reed-moor, as a peaceful region."

When the two pillars, the divine Izanagi and Izanami's augustness, younger sister and elder brother, had intercourse, and she had deigned to bear the many tens of countries of the countries, and the many tens of islands of the islands, and had deigned to bear the many hundred myriads of gods, she also deigned to bear her dear youngest child of all, the Fire-producer god, and her hidden parts being burnt, she hid in the rocks, and said: "My dear elder brother's augustness, deign not to look upon me for seven nights of nights and seven days of sunshine;" but when, before the seven days were fulfilled, he looked, thinking her remaining hidden to be strange, she deigned to say: "My hidden parts were burnt when I bore fire." At such a time I said, "My dear elder brother's augustness, deign not to look upon me, but you violently looked upon me;" and after saying, "My dear elder brother's augustness shall rule the upper country; I will rule the lower country." She deigned to hide in the rocks, and having come to the flat hill of darkness, she thought and said: "I have come hither, having born and left a bad-hearted child in the upper country, ruled over by my illustrious elder brother's augustness," and going back she bore other children. Having born the Water-goddess, the gourd, the river-weed, and the clay-hill maiden, four sorts of things, she taught them with words, and made them to know, saying: "If the heart of this bad-hearted child becomes violent, let the Water-goddess take the gourd, and the clay-hill maiden take the river-weed, and pacify him."

In consequence of this I fulfil his praises, and say that for the things set up, so that he may deign not to be awfully quick of heart in their great place of the Sovereign Grandchild's augustness, there are provided bright cloth, glittering cloth, soft cloth, and coarse cloth, and the five kinds of things; as to things which dwell in the blue sea plain, there are things wide of fin and things narrow of fin, down to the weeds of the offing and weeds of the shore; as to liquor, raising high the beer-jars, filling and ranging in rows the bellies of the beer-jars, piling the offerings up, even to rice in grain and rice in ear, like a range of hills, I fulfil his praises with the great ritual, the heavenly ritual.

RITUALS TO THE SUN-GODDESS

He (the priest envoy) says: "Hear all of you, ministers of the gods and sanctifiers of offerings, the great ritual, the Heavenly ritual, declared in the great presence of the Ffom-Heaven-shining-great deity, whose praises are fulfilled by setting up the stout pillars of the great house, and exalting the cross-beam to the plain of high Heaven at the sources of the Isuzu river at Udji in Watarahi."

He says: "It is the Sovereign's great Word. Hear all of you, ministers of the gods and sanctifiers of offerings, the fulfilling of praises on this seventeenth day of the sixth moon of this year, as the morning sun goes up in glory, of the Oho-Nakatomi, who-having abundantly piled up like a range of hills the tribute thread and sanctified liquor and food presented as of usage by the people of the deity's houses attributed to her in the three departments and in various countries and places, so that she deign to bless his (the Mikado's) life as a long life and his age as a luxuriant age eternally and unchangingly as multitudinous piles of rock; may deign to bless the children who are born to him, and deigning to cause to flourish the five kinds of grain which the men of a hundred functions and the peasants of the countries in the four quarters of the region under Heaven long and peacefully cultivate and eat, and guarding and benefiting them deign to bless them is hidden by the great offering-wands."

I declare in the great presence of the from-Heaven-shining-great deity who sits in Ise. Because the Sovereign great goddess bestows on him the countries of the four quarters over which her glance extends, as far as the limit where Heaven stands up like a wall, as far as the bounds where the country stands up distant, as far as the limit where the blue clouds spread flat, as far as the bounds where the white clouds lie away fallen. The blue sea plain as far as the limit whither come the prows of the ships without drying poles or paddles, the ships which continuously crowd on the great sea plain, and the roads which men travel by land, as far as the limit whither come the horses' hoofs, with the baggage-cords tied tightly, treading the uneven rocks and tree-roots and standing up continuously in a long path without a break -- making the narrow countries wide and the hilly countries plain, and as it were drawing together the distant countries by throwing many tens of ropes over them. He will pile up the first-fruits like a range of hills in the great presence of the Sovereign great goddess, and will peacefully enjoy the remainder.

THE HARVEST RITUAL

I declare in the presence of the sovereign gods of the Harvest, if the sovereign gods will bestow, in many-bundled spikes and in luxuriant spikes, the late-ripening harvest which they will bestow, the late-ripening harvest which will be produced by the dripping of foam from the arms, and by drawing the mud together between the opposing thighs, then I will fulfil their praises by presenting the first-fruits in a thousand ears, and in many hundred ears. Raising high the beer-jars, filling and ranging in rows the bellies of the beer-jars, I will present them in juice and in grain. As to things which grow in the great field plain--sweet herbs and bitter herbs; as to things which dwell in the blue sea plain--things wide of fin, and things narrow of fin, down to the weeds of the offing, and weeds of the shore; and as to Clothes, with bright cloth, glittering cloth, soft cloth, and coarse cloth will I fulfil their praises. And having furnished a white horse, a white boar, and a white cock, and the various kinds of things in the presence of the sovereign gods of the Harvest, I fulfil their praises by presenting the great Offerings of the sovereign Grand-child's augustness.

10

Zoroastrianism

The Avestas

FARGARD II

Yima (gamshêd).

The Zend Avesta, Part I from *Sacred Books of the East*, Volume 4, translated by James Darmesteter, (1880), sacred-texts.com

Ahura Mazda proposes to Yima, the son of Vîvanghat, to receive the law from him and to bring it to men. On his refusal, he bids him keep his creatures and make them prosper. Yima accordingly makes them thrive and increase, keeps death and disease away from them, and three times enlarges the earth, which had become too narrow for its inhabitants.

1. Zarathustra asked Ahura Mazda:

    O Ahura Mazda, most beneficent Spirit, Maker of the material world, thou Holy One!
    Who was the first mortal, before myself, Zarathustra, with whom thou, Ahura Mazda, didst converse, whom thou didst teach the law of Ahura, the law of Zarathustra?

2. Ahura Mazda answered:

    The fair Yima, the great shepherd, O holy Zarathustra! he was the first mortal, before thee, Zarathustra, with whom I, Ahura Mazda, did converse, whom I taught the law of Ahura, the law of Zarathustra.

3. Unto him, O Zarathustra, I, Ahura Mazda, spake, saying: 'Well, fair Yima, son of Vîvanghat, be thou the preacher and the bearer of my law!'

    And the fair Yima, O Zarathustra, replied unto me, saying:
    'I was not born, I was not taught to be the preacher and the bearer of thy law.'

4. Then I, Ahura Mazda, said thus unto him, O Zarathustra:

   'Since thou wantest not to be the preacher and the bearer of my law, then make thou my worlds thrive, make my worlds increase: undertake thou to nourish, to rule, and to watch over my world.'

5. And the fair Yima replied unto me, O Zarathustra, saying:

   'Yes! I will make thy worlds thrive, I will make thy worlds increase. Yes! I will nourish, and rule, and watch over thy world. There shall be, while I am king, neither cold wind nor hot wind, neither disease nor death.'

7. Then I, Ahura Mazda, brought two implements unto him: a golden ring and a poniard inlaid with gold. Behold, here Yima bears the royal sway!

8. Thus, under the sway of Yima, three hundred winters passed away, and the earth was replenished with flocks and herds, with men and dogs and birds and with red blazing fires, and there was no more room for flocks, herds, and men.

pp. 11-13

Vendîdâd Sâdah

FARGARD XII

If one's father or mother dies, how long shall they stay [2], the son for the father, the daughter for her mother? How long for the righteous? How long for the sinners [3]? Ahura Mazda answered: 'They shall stay thirty days for the righteous, sixty days for the sinners.' O Maker of the material world, thou Holy One! How shall I cleanse the house? How shall it be clean again? Ahura Mazda answered: 'They shall wash their bodies three times, they shall wash their clothes three times, they shall chant the Gâthas three times; they shall offer up a sacrifice to my Fire, they shall offer up the bundles of baresma, they shall bring libations to the good waters; then the house shall be clean, and then the waters may enter, then the fire may enter, and then the Amesha-Spentas may enter [4], O Spitama Zarathustra!'

FARGARD XX.

Thrita, the First Healer.

Thrita was the first who drove back death and disease, as Ahura Mazda had brought to him down from heaven ten thousand healing plants that had been growing up around the tree of eternal life, the white Hôm or Gaokerena. Thrita is mentioned only once again in the Avesta, in Yasna IX, 7, where he appears to have been one of the first priests of Haoma. This accounts for his medical skill; as Haoma is a source of life and health, his first priests must have been the first healers.

1. Zarathustra asked Ahura Mazda: 'Ahura Mazda, most beneficent Spirit, Maker of the material world, thou Holy One! Who was he who first of the healthful, the wise, the happy, the wealthy, the glorious, the strong men of yore, drove back sickness to sickness, drove back death to death, and first turned away the point of the poniard and the fire of fever from the bodies of mortals.'

2. Ahura Mazda answered: 'Thrita it was who first of the healthful, the wise, the happy, the wealthy, the glorious, the strong man of yore, drove back sickness to sickness, drove back death to death, and first turned away the point of the poniard and the fire of fever from the bodies of mortals.

3. 'He asked for a source of remedies; he obtained it from Khshathra-Vairya, to withstand sickness and to withstand death, to withstand pain and fever, to withstand the disease, rottenness and infection which Angra Mainyu (a.k.a. Ahriman or the force of evil) had created witchcraft against the bodies of mortals.

4. 'And I Ahura Mazda brought down the healing plants that, by many hundreds, by many thousands, by many myriads, grow up all around the one Gaokerena.

5. 'All this (health) do we call by our blessing-spells, by our prayers, by our praises, upon the bodies of mortals.

7. 'To thee, O Sickness, I say avaunt (go away)! to thee, O Death, I say avaunt (go away)! to thee, O Pain, I say avaunt (go away)! to thee, O Fever, I say avaunt (go away)! to thee, O Disease, I say avaunt (go away)!'

pp. 220-221

Zoroastrian Invocation
(Recited Before the Reading of Scriptures)

May Ahura Mazda be rejoiced! . . .

Ashem Vohû: Holiness is the best of all good . . . .

I confess myself a worshipper of Mazda, a follower of Zarathustra, one who hates the Daêvas and obeys the laws of Ahura;

For sacrifice, prayer, propitiation, and glorification unto [Hâvani], the holy and master of holiness . . .

Unto Haurvatât, the master; unto the prosperity of the seasons and unto the years, the masters of holiness,

Be propitiation, with sacrifice, prayer, propitiation, and glorification.

Yathâ ahû vairyô: The will of the Lord is the law of holiness . . . .

We sacrifice unto Haurvatât, the Amesha-Spenta; we sacrifice unto the prosperity of the seasons; we sacrifice unto the years, the holy and masters of holiness.

Zend Avesta

YASNA XII

THE MAZDAYASNIAN CONFESSION

The Zend Avesta, Part III, from *Sacred Books of the East*, Volume 4, translated by L.H. Mills, (1886 at sacred-texts.com

And so I myself, in whatsoever circumstances I may be placed, as a worshipper of Mazda, and of Zarathustra's order, would so abjure the Daêvas and their shelter, as he who was the holy Zarathustra abjured them (once of old).

7. To that religious sanctity to which the waters appertain, do I belong, to that sanctity to which the plants, to that sanctity to which the cattle of blessed gift, to that religious sanctity to which Ahura Mazda, who made both cattle and holy men, belongs, to that sanctity do I. Of that creed which Zarathustra held, which Kavi Vîstâspa, and those two, Frashaostra and Gâmâspa; yea, of that religious faith which every Saoshyant who shall (yet come to) save (us), the holy ones who do the deeds of real significance, of that creed, and of that lore, am I.

8. A Mazda-worshipper I am, of Zarathustra's order; (so) do I confess, as a praiser and confessor, and I therefore praise aloud the well-thought thought, the word well spoken, and the deed well done;

9. Yea, I praise at once the Faith of Mazda, the Faith which has no faltering utterance, the Faith that wields the felling halbert blade, the Faith of kindred marriage, the holy (Creed), which is the most imposing, best, and most beautiful of all religions which exist, and of all that shall in future come to knowledge, Ahura's Faith, the Zarathustrian creed. Yea, to Ahura Mazda do I ascribe all good, and such shall be the worship of the Mazdayasnian belief!

pp. 249-250

11

Judaism

Genesis 1 – 3: The Creation Stories

Introduction by Danya Furda (2016)

Genesis (Bereshit), the first book in the Hebrew Bible or Old Testament, opens with two accounts of creation. The first one from Genesis 1:1 – 2:4a is the newer account written from the Priestly source. [According to the documentary hypothesis, there are four independent sources for the Torah, the first five books of the Hebrew Bible. These four are the Yahwist or Jahwist (J), the Elohist (E), the Deuteronomist (D) and the Priestly writer (P)]. The liturgical nature of this account is reflected in the common refrain, "And there was evening, and there was morning – the X day." In this account, God, who is referred to as Elohim, "speaks" the universe into being on the sixth day, and at the same time creates humans in his image. Because God rests on the seventh day from his creative work, Jews as well are to rest, do no work, and keep sacred the Sabbath (Shabbat) from sundown on Friday until sundown on Saturday.

Genesis 2:4b – 2:25 is the second account of creation in which God, here called Yahweh Elohim, physically creates a garden, animals and the first humans. God is also described in humanistic terms, as talking and walking in his garden. He forms man ("Adam," meaning earthling) out of the ground and then later forms woman out of the rib or side of Adam. The purpose of this story is to explain why there is sin, suffering and hardship, patriarchy, and death in the world. This creation story is likely based on an oral folk tradition that was later written down and represents a more ancient version than that of the first creation account. It comes from the Yahwist (J) source.

Chapter 1 – ¹In the beginning God created the heavens and the earth. ²Now the earth was formless and empty, darkness was over the surface of the deep, and the Spirit of the God was hovering over the waters. ³And God said, "Let there be light," and there was light. ⁴God saw that the light was good, and he separated the light from the darkness. ⁵God called the light "day," and the darkness he called "night." And there was evening, and there was morning -- the first day.

[6]And God said, "Let there be a vault between the waters to separate water from water." [7]So God made the vault and separated the water under the vault from the water above it. And it was so. [8]God called the vault "sky." And there was evening, and there was morning -- the second day.

[9]And God said, "Let the water under the sky be gathered to one place, and let the dry ground appear. " And it was so. [10]God called the dry ground "land," and the gathered waters he called "seas." And God saw that it was good. [11]Then God said, "Let the land produce vegetation: seed-bearing plants and trees on the land that bear fruit with seed in it, according to their various kinds." And it was so. [12]The land produced vegetation: plants bearing seed according to their kinds and trees bearing fruit with seed in it according to their kinds. And God saw that it was good. [13]And there was evening, and there was morning -- the third day.

[14]And God said, "Let there be lights in the vault of the sky to separate the day from the nights, and let them serve as signs to mark sacred times, and days and years, [15]and let them be lights in the vault of the sky to give light to the earth." And it was so. [16]God made two great lights -- the greater light to govern the day and the lesser light to govern the night. He also made the stars. [17]God set them in the vault of the sky to give light to the earth, [18]to govern the day and the night, and to separate light from darkness. And God saw that it was good. [19]And there was evening, and there was morning -- the fourth day.

[20]And God said, "Let the water teem with living creatures, and let birds fly above the earth across the vault of the sky." [21]So God created the great creatures of the sea and every living thing with which the water teems and that moves about in it, according to their kinds, and every winged bird according to its kind. And God saw that it was good. [22]God blessed them and said, "Be fruitful and increase in numbers and filled the water in the seas, and let the birds increase on the earth." [23]And there was evening, and there was morning -- the fifth day.

[24]And God said, "Let the land produce living creatures according to their kinds: the livestock, the creatures that move along the ground, and the wild animals, each according to its kind." And it was so. [25]God made the wild animals according to their kinds, the livestock according to their kinds, and all the creatures that move along the ground according to their kinds. And God saw that it was good. [26]Then God said, "Let us make mankind in our image, in our likeness, so that they may rule over the fish in the sea and the birds in the sky, over the livestock and all the wild animals, and over all the creatures

that move along the ground." ²⁷So God created mankind in his own image, in the image of God he created them; male and female he created them. ²⁸God blessed them and said to them, "Be fruitful and increase in number; fill the earth and subdue it. Rule over the fish in the sea and the birds in the sky and over every living creature that moved on the ground." ²⁹Then God said, "I give you every seed-bearing plant on the face of the whole earth and every tree that has fruit with seed in it. They will be yours for food. ³⁰And to all the beasts of the earth and all the birds in the sky and all the creatures that move along the ground -- everything that has the breath of life in it -- I give every green plant for food." And it was so. ³¹God saw all that he had made, and it was very good. And there was evening, and there was morning -- the sixth day.

Chapter 2 – ¹Thus the heavens and the earth were completed in all their vast array. ²By the seventh day God had finished the work he had been doing; so on the seventh day he rested from all his work. ³Then God blessed the seventh day and made it holy, because on it he rested from all the work of creating that he had done.

⁴This is the account of the heavens and the earth when they were created.

The Lord God made the earth and the heavens. ⁵Now no shrub had yet appeared on the earth and no plant had yet sprung up, for the Lord God had not sent rain on the earth and there was no one to work the ground, ⁶but streams came up from the earth and watered the whole surface of the ground. ⁷Then the Lord God formed a man from the dust of the ground and breathed into his nostrils the breath of life, and the man became a living being.

⁸Now the Lord God had planted a garden in the east, in Eden; and there he put the man he had formed. ⁹The Lord God made all kinds of trees grow out of the ground -- trees that were pleasing to the eye and good for food. In the middle of the garden were the tree of life and the tree of the knowledge of good and evil.

¹⁰A river watering the garden flowed from Eden: from there it was separated into four headwaters. ¹¹The name of the first is the Pishon; it winds through the entire land of Havilah, where there is gold. ¹²(The god of that land is good; aromatic resin and onyx are also there.) ¹³The name of the second river is the Gihon; it winds through the entire land of Cush. ¹⁴The name of the third river is the Tigris; it runs along the east side of Ashur. And the fourth river is the Euphrates.

¹⁵The Lord God took the man and put him in the garden of Eden to work it and take care of it. ¹⁶And the Lord God commanded the man, "You are free to eat from any tree in the garden, ¹⁷but you must not eat from the tree of the knowledge of good and evil, for when you eat from it you will certainly die.

¹⁸The Lord God said, "It is not good for the man to be alone. I will make a helper suitable for him."

¹⁹Now the Lord God had formed out of the ground all the wild animals and all the birds in the sky. He brought them to the man to see what he would name them; and whatever the man called each living creature, that was its name. ²⁰So the man gave names to all the livestock, the birds in the sky and all the wild animals.

But for the man no suitable helper was found. ²¹So the Lord God caused the man to fall into a deep sleep; and while he was sleeping, he took one of the man's ribs and then closed up the place with flesh. ²²Then the Lord God made a woman from the rib he had taken out of the man, and he brought her to the man.

²³The man said,

"This is now bone of my bones
and flesh of my flesh;
she shall be called 'woman,'
for she was taken out of man."

²⁴That is why a man leaves his father and mother and is united to his wife, and they become one flesh. ²⁵Adam and his wife were both naked, and they felt no shame.

Chapter 3 – ¹Now the serpent was craftier than any of the wild animals the Lord God had made. He said to the woman, "Did God really say, 'You must not eat from any tree in the garden'?" ²The woman said to the serpent, "We may eat fruit from the trees in the garden, ³but God did say, 'you must not eat fruit from the tree that is in the middle of the garden, and you must not touch it, or you will die.'"

⁴"You will not die," the serpent said to the woman, ⁵"for God knows that when you eat from it, your eyes will be opened, and you will be like God, knowing good and evil."

⁶When the woman saw that the fruit of the tree was good for food and pleasing to the eye, and also desirable for gaining wisdom, she took some and ate it. She also gave some to her husband, who was with her, and he ate it. ⁷Then the eyes of both of them were opened, and they realized they were naked; so they sewed fig leaves together and made coverings for themselves.

⁸Then the man and his wife heard the sound of the Lord God as he was walking in the garden in the cool of the day, and they hid from the Lord God among the trees of the garden. ⁹But the Lord God called to the man, "Where are you?" ¹⁰He answered, "I heard you in the garden, and I was afraid because I was naked, so I hid." ¹¹And he said, "Who told you that you were naked? Have you eaten from the tree that I commanded you not to eat from?" ¹²The man said, "The women you put here with me -- she gave me some fruit from the tree, and I ate it." ¹³Then the Lord God said to the woman, "What is this you have done?" The woman said, "The serpent deceived me, and I ate."

¹⁴So the Lord God said to the serpent,
"Because you have done this,
Cursed are you above all livestock and all the wild animals!
You will crawl on your belly and you will eat dust all the days of your life.

¹⁵And I will put enmity between you and the woman, between your offspring and hers;
He will crush you head, and you will strike his heel."

¹⁶To the woman he said,
"I will make your pains in childbearing very severe;
With painful labor you will give birth to children.
Your desire will be for your husband, and he will rule over you."

¹⁷To Adam he said,
"Because you listened to your wife
And ate fruit from the tree about which I commanded you, 'You must not eat from it,'
Cursed is the ground because of you;
Through painful toil you will eat food from it all the days of your life.
¹⁸It will produce thorns and thistles for you, and you will eat the plants of the field.
By the sweat of your brow you will eat your food until you return to the ground,

Since from it you were taken;
For dust you are and to dust you will return."

¹⁸Adam named his wife Eve, because she would become the mother of all the living. ¹⁹The Lord God made garments of skin for Adam and his wife and clothed them.

²²And the Lord God said, "The man has now become like one of us, knowing good and evil. He must not be allowed to reach out his hand and take also from the tree of life and eat and live forever." ²³So the Lord God banished him from the garden of Eden to work the ground from which he had been taken. ²⁴After he drove the man out, he placed on the east side of the garden of Eden cherubim and a flaming sword flashing back and forth to guard the way to the tree of life.

The Covenant and the Law, Selections from Exodus

Introduction by Mark Bocija

> *The Jewish Scriptures, some thirty-nine books, date from the tenth to the first century BCE. and are arranged into three categories: the Torah, the Prophets, and the Writings. The Torah (or Law), according to tradition the work of Moses, is the most authoritative part of the scriptures because it provides the standards of behavior for everyday life. The Prophets are the written accounts of the lives and teachings of individuals who were understood to speak for God himself at critical times in the history of the Jewish people. The Writings, while they lack the theological and moral authority of the Torah and the Prophets, are deeply personal and sometimes moving accounts of individuals wrestling with feelings of guilt, doubt, faith, and uncertainty. The variety of genres and the span of time in which the Jewish Bible was conceived belie the underlying unity of the collection. The Jewish Scriptures as a whole represent an on-going effort to comprehend who and what God is, how God interacts with creation and the human community throughout history, human nature, our place in the universe, and what God demands of us as we go through life.*

> *One of the central developments of Hebrew religion was the notion of covenant. In Mesopotamian religion, suffering was inevitable. The gods were capricious and unpredictable and humans bore the brunt of their anger. The Hebrews came to see God as merciful. He created a cosmic order that was intended to be beneficial to humankind. Part of that order was the Law. Human choices to violate God's law are the source of human misfortune. According to Hebrew*

tradition, God chose the Hebrews as his people to live according to the covenant, or sacred agreement. As long as they live by the covenant, they would live well. This sense of confidence in the goodness and mercy of God, combined with the recognition of their own responsibility to live according to God's law, is the centerpiece of the Hebrew idea of covenant. A recurring theme in the following selections is that since God rescued the Hebrew people from unjust oppression, they are obliged to commemorate God's mercy by acting justly in their dealing with others.

In the third month after their departure from the land of Egypt, on its first day, the Israelites came to the desert of Sinai. After the journey from Rephidim to the desert of Sinai, they pitched camp. While Israel was encamped here in front of the mountain, Moses went up the mountain to God. Then the LORD called to him and said, "Thus shall you say to the house of Jacob; tell the Israelites: You have seen for yourselves how I treated the Egyptians and how I bore you up on eagle wings and brought you here to myself. Therefore, if you hearken to my voice and keep my covenant, you shall be my special possession, dearer to me than all other people, though all the earth is mine." (Exodus 19)

Then God delivered all these commandments:

"I, the LORD, am your God, who brought you out of the land of Egypt, that place of slavery.

You shall not have other gods besides me.

You shall not carve idols for yourselves in the shape of anything in the sky above or on the earth below or in the waters beneath the earth; you shall not bow down before them or worship them. For I, the LORD, your God, am a jealous God, inflicting punishment for their fathers' wickedness on the children of those who hate me, down to the third and fourth generation; but bestowing mercy down to the thousandth generation, on the children of those who love me and keep my commandments.

"You shall not take the name of the LORD, your God, in vain. For the LORD will not leave unpunished him who takes his name in vain.

"Remember to keep holy the Sabbath day. Six days you may labor and do all your work, but the seventh day is the sabbath of the LORD, your God. No work may be done then either by you, or your son or daughter, or your male or female slave, or your beast, or by the alien who lives with you. In six days the LORD made the heavens and the earth, the sea and all that is in them; but on the seventh day he rested. That is why the LORD has blessed the sabbath day and made it holy.

"Honor your father and your mother, that you may have a long life in the land which the LORD, your God, is giving you.

"You shall not kill.

"You shall not commit adultery.

"You shall not steal.

"You shall not bear false witness against your neighbor.

"You shall not covet your neighbor's house. You shall not covet your neighbor's wife, nor his male or female slave, nor his ox or ass, nor anything else that belongs to him."

When the people witnessed the thunder and lightning, the trumpet blast and the mountain smoking, they all feared and trembled. So they took up a position much farther away

and said to Moses, "You speak to us, and we will listen; but let not God speak to us, or we shall die." Moses answered the people, "Do not be afraid, for God has come to you only to test you and put his fear upon you, lest you should sin." Still the people remained at a distance, while Moses approached the cloud where God was. The LORD told Moses, "Thus shall you speak to the Israelites: You have seen for yourselves that I have spoken to you from heaven.

Do not make anything to rank with me; neither gods of silver nor gods of gold shall you make for yourselves. An altar of earth you shall make for me, and upon it you shall sacrifice your holocausts and peace offerings, your sheep and your oxen. In whatever place I choose for the remembrance of my name I will come to you and bless you. If you make an altar of stone for me, do not build it of cut stone, for by putting a tool to it you desecrate it. You shall not go up by steps to my altar, on which you must not be indecently uncovered."

The Application of the Law;
Leviticus and Deuteronomy

Introduction by Mark Bocija

Like the Babylonians, the Hebrews found it necessary to expand upon customs and basic legal traditions in order to create a workable social order. Hebrew and Israelite law incorporated many of the themes and legal codes of earlier cultures. As in the code of Hammurabi, laws tend to focus on economic, social, and political relationships. However, the laws tend to be less retributive in nature. More important than retribution or order is the concept of justice. Hebrew law seems to be more concerned with people than with property. [1] *The Hebrews also rejected the idea of a legally stratified society with different values placed on nobles and commoners. The recognition that at one time all of them were slaves seems to have been an important factor in limiting the significance of status and encouraging a sense of equality and social responsibility.*

Leviticus 19

"When you reap the harvest of your land, you shall not be so thorough that you reap the field to its very edge, nor shall you glean the stray ears of grain. Likewise, you shall not pick your vineyard bare, nor gather up the grapes that have fallen. These things you shall leave for the poor and the alien. I, the LORD, am your God.

"You shall not steal. You shall not lie or speak falsely to one another. You shall not swear falsely by my name, thus profaning the name of your God. I am the LORD.

"You shall not defraud or rob your neighbor. You shall not withhold overnight the wages of your day laborer. You shall not curse the deaf, or put a stumbling block in front of the blind, but you shall fear your God. I am the LORD.

"You shall not act dishonestly in rendering judgment. Show neither partiality to the weak nor deference to the mighty, but judge your fellow men justly. You shall not go about spreading slander among your kinsmen; nor shall you stand by idly when your neighbor's life is at stake. I am the LORD.

---

1   Perry, *Sources of the Western Tradition (2011)*

"You shall not bear hatred for your brother in your heart. Though you may have to reprove your fellow man, do not incur sin because of him. Take no revenge and cherish no grudge against your fellow countrymen. You shall love your neighbor as yourself. I am the LORD."

"When an alien resides with you in your land, do not molest him. You shall treat the alien who resides with you no differently than the natives born among you; have the same love for him as for yourself; for you too were once aliens in the land of Egypt. I, the LORD, am your God.

"Do not act dishonestly in using measures of length or weight or capacity. You shall have a true scale and true weights, an honest ephah and an honest hin. I, the LORD, am your God, who brought you out of the land of Egypt. Be careful, then, to observe all my statutes and decrees. I am the LORD."

Deuteronomy 24

"When you make a loan of any kind to your neighbor, you shall not enter his house to receive a pledge from him, but shall wait outside until the man to whom you are making the loan brings his pledge outside to you. If he is a poor man, you shall not sleep in the mantle he gives as a pledge, but shall return it to him at sunset that he himself may sleep in it. Then he will bless you, and it will be a good deed of yours before the LORD, your God.

"You shall not defraud a poor and needy hired servant, whether he be one of your own countrymen or one of the aliens who live in your communities. You shall pay him each day's wages before sundown on the day itself, since he is poor and looks forward to them. Otherwise he will cry to the LORD against you, and you will be held guilty.

"Fathers shall not be put to death for their children, nor children for their fathers; only for his own guilt shall a man be put to death.

"You shall not violate the rights of the alien or of the orphan, nor take the clothing of a widow as a pledge. For, remember, you were once slaves in Egypt, and the LORD, your God, ransomed you from there; that is why I command you to observe this rule.

"When you reap the harvest in your field and overlook a sheaf there, you shall not go back to get it; let it be for the alien, the orphan or the widow, that the LORD, your God, may bless you in all your undertakings. When you knock down the fruit of your olive trees, you shall not go over the branches a second time; let what remains be for the alien, the orphan and the widow.

"When you pick your grapes, you shall not go over the vineyard a second time; let what remains be for the alien, the orphan, and the widow. For remember that you were once slaves in Egypt; that is why I command you to observe this rule."

The Prophets, Social Justice and Universal Humanity

Introduction and comments for Amos, Isiah, and Psalms by Mark Bocija.

The Hebrews' belief in a single God whose nature was "goodness" and who desired good for his creation led ancient Judaism to evolve a religious outlook that we call "ethical monotheism," which becomes the foundation for the three great Western religions--Judaism, Christianity, and Islam. At the core of this tradition is the belief that God requires more of the individual than ritual propriety. God requires each individual to act as an agent of justice. The notion of the individual as a moral agent with a responsibility to God was the most prominent theme of the prophetic movement that began in the eighth century. The prophets emphasized God's demand for individual ethical behavior even over ritual sacrifice. Their insistence that there is a moral imperative to care for the poor and guarantee justice becomes an integral part of the Western ideal of social justice. The word "prophet" literally means to "speak for" someone. Prophets such as Amos and Isaiah spoke in the first person as the voice of God. Their demands for righteousness were accompanied by dire warnings of divine retribution if the people would not divert from their selfish ways. The prophet Amos's thundering demand for justice was a favorite of civil rights leader, Martin Luther King, Jr.

Amos (5:1-24)

Hear this word which I utter over you, a lament, O house of Israel:

She is fallen, to rise no more, the virgin Israel; she lies abandoned upon her land, with no one to raise her up. Woe to those who turn judgment to

103

wormwood and cast justice to the ground![2] They hate him who reproves at the gate and abhor him who speaks the truth. Therefore, because you have trampled upon the weak and exacted of them levies of grain, though you have built houses of hewn stone, you shall not live in them! Though you have planted choice vineyards, you shall not drink their wine! Yes, I know how many are your crimes, how grievous your sins: Oppressing the just, accepting bribes, repelling the needy at the gate!

Seek good and not evil, that you may live; then truly will the LORD, the God of hosts, be with you as you claim! Hate evil and love good, and let justice prevail at the gate; then it may be that the LORD, the God of hosts, will have pity on the remnant of Joseph.[3] Therefore, thus says the LORD, the God of hosts: In every square there shall be lamentation, and in every street they shall cry, Alas! Alas! They shall summon the farmers to wail and professional mourners to lament, and in every vineyard there shall be lamentation when I pass through your midst, says the LORD. Woe to those who yearn for the day of the LORD! What will this day of the LORD mean for you? Darkness and not light! As if a man went to flee from a lion, and a bear should meet him; or as if on entering his house he were to rest his hand against the wall, and a snake should bite him. Will not the day of the LORD be darkness and not light, gloom without any brightness?

I hate, I detest your feasts, and I take no pleasure in your solemn assemblies. [4]Your cereal offerings I will not accept, nor will I consider the offerings of fatted beasts. Away with your noisy songs! I will not listen to the melodies of your harps. But if you would offer me holocausts [5], then let justice flow like water, and righteousness like an unfailing stream[6].

---

2   "I am in Birmingham because injustice is here. Just as the prophets of the eighth century B.C. left their villages and carried their 'thus saith the Lord' far beyond the boundaries of their home towns . . . . Was not Amos an extremist for justice – 'Let justice roll down like waters and righteousness like a mighty stream.'" – *Letter from a Birmingham Jail*

3   Joseph was the eleventh son of Jacob through Rachel in the Book of Genesis and the founder of the tribes Ephraim and Manasseh. Terms like the "remnant of Joseph" and the "house of Joseph" are common metaphors for the people of Israel.

4   Amos is referring to the rituals of the Temple that, just as in other Ancient Near Eastern religions, were performed to please God and so win his favor.

5   A sacrifice that is burned so that the deity can consume its smoke.

6   This was King's quote from Amos in the famous "I Have a Dream" speech.

Isaiah (19: 23-24)

While the prophets foretold of the punishment that God had in store for the wicked, they also held out hope for the deliverance of humankind from war and suffering. The passages from Isaiah reflect a growing universalism in Hebrew thought. While Yahweh had chosen the Hebrews to be his agents, all human beings are children of the same God and destined to live in peace and brotherhood.

On that day there shall be a highway from Egypt to Assyria; the Assyrians shall enter Egypt, and the Egyptians enter Assyria, and Egypt shall serve Assyria.

On that day Israel shall be a third party with Egypt and Assyria, a blessing in the midst of the land, when the LORD of hosts blesses it: "Blessed be my people Egypt, and the work of my hands Assyria, and my inheritance, Israel."

Isaiah (2:1-5)

This is what Isaiah, son of Amoz, saw concerning Judah and Jerusalem.

In days to come, the mountain of the LORD'S house shall be established as the highest mountain and raised above the hills. All nations shall stream toward it; many peoples shall come and say: "Come, let us climb the LORD'S mountain, to the house of the God of Jacob, that he may instruct us in his ways, and we may walk in his paths." For from Zion shall go forth instruction, and the word of the LORD from Jerusalem.

He shall judge between the nations, and impose terms on many peoples. They shall beat their swords into plowshares and their spears into pruning hooks; one nation shall not raise the sword against another, nor shall they train for war again.

O house of Jacob, come, let us walk in the light of the LORD!

Writings: Selections from Psalms and Job

Psalms, Chapter 51

The following selection is the one of the most famous of all the psalms. According to tradition, it was written by King David after he was confronted by the prophet, Nathan. David had committed adultery with and impregnated the beautiful Bathsheba, the wife of Uriah the Hittite. To cover up his crime, he arranged the death of her husband and then married her. David's lament in Psalm 51 is a profound psychological portrait of a man tormented by the guilt of his actions. Yet, this is a more a song of hope than it is one of despair. The recognition of his failure is accompanied by the hope for healing and redemption.

Have mercy on me, God, in your goodness; in your abundant compassion blot out my offense.

Wash away all my guilt; from my sin cleanse me.

For I know my offense; my sin is always before me.

Against you alone have I sinned; I have done such evil in your sight that you are just in your sentence, blameless when you condemn.

[7]True, I was born guilty, a sinner, even as my mother conceived me.

Still, you insist on sincerity of heart; in my inmost being teach me wisdom.

Cleanse me with hyssop[8], that I may be pure; wash me, make me whiter than snow.

Let me hear sounds of joy and gladness; let the bones you have crushed rejoice.

---

7   This is not a reference to the notion of original sin, which was introduced by Paul (Romans 5:12–21 and 1 Corinthians 15:22) and further articulatedby later Christian writers such as Tertullian, Cyprian, Ambrose, and most famously Augustine. Here, it should be read as a reflection of the psalmist's personal feelings of guilt and self-loathing.

8   Hyssop is a bush. People were not actually cleansed with it, but because hyssop has many small branches, it was ideal for dipping in liquid and sprinkling objects. He is probably referring to the practice of using a hyssop branch to sprinkle water on things as a way of ritually cleansing them. In the book of Numbers, "For anyone who is thus unclean, ashes from the sin offering shall be put in a vessel, and spring water shall be poured on them. Then a man who is clean shall take some hyssop, dip it in this water, and sprinkle it on the tent and on all the vessels and persons that were in it, or on him who touched a bone, a slain person or other dead body, or a grave.

Turn away your face from my sins; blot out all my guilt.

A clean heart create for me, God; renew in me a steadfast spirit.

Do not drive me from your presence, nor take from me your holy spirit.

Restore my joy in your salvation [9]; sustain in me a willing spirit.

I will teach the wicked your ways, that sinners may return to you.

Rescue me from death, God, my saving God, that my tongue may praise your healing power.

Lord, open my lips; my mouth will proclaim your praise.

For you do not desire sacrifice; a burnt offering you would not accept.

My sacrifice, God, is a broken spirit; God, do not spurn a broken, humbled heart.

Make Zion prosper in your good pleasure; rebuild the walls of Jerusalem.

Then you will be pleased with proper sacrifice, burnt offerings and holocausts; then bullocks will be offered on your altar.

Book of Job (19:1-29)

Selections from the Book of Job, World English Bible
Introduced and emended by Sue Burnam. Initial introductory comments by Mark Bocija

> *The Book of Job is a long, dramatic poem that addresses the problem of human suffering. Job, the protagonist of the story, is a pious and upright man, "blameless" before God, prosperous and happy with many children. Then Job suffers a complete reversal of fortune. His family is killed and his property is taken from him. He is afflicted by a loathsome disease and is in constant agony. Having lost everything, he curses the day he was born. His friends, who have come to console him, suggest that perhaps he is being punished for some offence against God, but Job protests his innocence. He calls for God himself to explain the cause of his suffering. But God's answer to Job is not an explanation or justification of why good people suffer. It is rather a statement of God's own*

---

9   This is not a reference to eternal life. There is no doctrine of the afterlife in Hebrew religion.

omnipotence. Job, humbled, must learn that in this world even the good may suffer. Suffering is a test and fidelity will be rewarded in the end. As readers we look in vain for a satisfactory explanation that will make the suffering of innocent people seem reasonable and acceptable. The author of Job is far too subtle to offer answers. Instead, Job's desperate desire to understand why he suffers offers not an explanation, but a shared experience of a common humanity. The story holds out hope that human suffering is not random and meaningless, and that steadfastness and faith in God will bring renewal.

The Book of Job tells the story of a righteous man who suffers. Job is a pious man whose devotion to God is subjected to a series of tests. "The Satan," who in this case is an adversary or accuser, not the fallen angel figure of later tales, suggests to God that Job is only devoted because God has been so good to him. Will his faith remain steadfast if the good life he has been living is stripped away from him? As his suffering increases, Job maintains his faith while continuing to demand an explanation. In the end, he is confronted with the power of God, and that is his answer. God restores Job's good life.

The test arranged between God and the Adversary and the restoration of Job's fortune at the end of the book are described in prose passages. The prose sections frame a long poetic narrative of the various trials of Job, his friends' reactions, his questioning, and the response of God.

The central issue is the existence of suffering in a world created by a good God. The term "theodicy" refers to efforts to justify the presence of evil in a world ruled by a God who is entirely good and entirely powerful. Is suffering justified because Job must have deserved it? Is he suffering because members of his family must have done something wrong? Is his suffering justified as a test of his devotion? Various explanations are given in the course of the story, and many interpretations are possible.

A righteous man

There was a man in the land of Uz, whose name was Job. That man was blameless and upright, and one who feared God and turned away from evil. There were born to him seven sons and three daughters. His possessions also were seven thousand sheep, three thousand camels, five hundred yoke of oxen, five hundred female donkeys, and a very great household; so that this man was the greatest of all the children of the east. His sons went and held a feast in the house of each one on his birthday; and they sent and called for their three sisters to eat and to drink with them. It was so, when the days of their feasting had run their course, that Job sent and sanctified them, and rose up early in the morning, and offered burnt offerings according to the number of them all. For Job said, "It may be that my sons have sinned, and renounced God in their hearts." Job did so continually.

God and Satan consider the case of Job

Now on the day when God's sons came to present themselves before Yahweh, Satan also came among them. Yahweh said to Satan, "Where have you come from?"

Then Satan answered Yahweh, and said, "From going back and forth in the earth, and from walking up and down in it."

Yahweh said to Satan, "Have you considered my servant, Job? For there is no one like him in the earth, a blameless and an upright man, one who fears God, and turns away from evil."

Then Satan answered Yahweh, and said, "Does Job fear God for nothing? Haven't you made a hedge around him, and around his house, and around all that he has, on every side? You have blessed the work of his hands, and his substance is increased in the land. But stretch out your hand now, and touch all that he has, and he will renounce you to your face."

Yahweh said to Satan, "Behold, all that he has is in your power. Only on himself don't stretch out your hand."

So Satan went out from the presence of Yahweh. It fell on a day when his sons and his daughters were eating and drinking wine in their oldest brother's house, that there came a messenger to Job, and said, "The oxen were plowing, and the donkeys feeding beside them, and the Sabeans attacked, and took them away. Yes, they have killed the servants with the edge of the sword, and I alone have escaped to tell you."

While he was still speaking, there also came another, and said, "The fire of God has fallen from the sky, and has burned up the sheep and the servants, and consumed them, and I alone have escaped to tell you."

[Again enemies come and destroy Job's possessions, and a windstorm kills Job's sons and daughters.]

Then Job arose, and tore his robe, and shaved his head, and fell down on the ground, and worshiped. He said, "Naked I came out of my mother's womb, and naked will I return there. Yahweh gave, and Yahweh has taken away. Blessed be Yahweh's name." In all this, Job didn't sin, nor charge God with wrongdoing.

God agrees to further trials for Job

[Satan] said, "Skin for skin. Yes, all that a man has he will give for his life. But stretch out your hand now, and touch his bone and his flesh, and he will renounce you to your face."

Yahweh said to Satan, "Behold, he is in your hand. Only spare his life."

So Satan went out from the presence of Yahweh, and struck Job with painful sores from the sole of his foot to his head. He took for himself a potsherd to scrape himself with, and he sat among the ashes. Then his wife said to him, "Do you still maintain your integrity? Renounce God, and die."

But he said to her, "You speak as one of the foolish women would speak. What? Shall we receive good at the hand of God, and shall we not receive evil?"

Job's friends seek to explain this suffering

In all this Job didn't sin with his lips. Now when Job's three friends heard of all this evil that had come on him, they each came from his own place: Eliphaz the Temanite, Bildad the Shuhite, and Zophar the Naamathite; and they made an appointment together to come to sympathize with him and to comfort him. When they lifted up their eyes from a distance, and didn't recognize him, they raised their voices, and wept; and they each tore his robe, and sprinkled dust on their heads toward the sky. So they sat down with him on the ground seven days and seven nights, and no one spoke a word to him, for they saw that his grief was very great.

[Job's friends suggest that he must deserve this suffering, since God does not punish the innocent. Perhaps Job's children have sinned against God. Perhaps Job deserves far worse, and God is being merciful. If Job will repent, God will forgive him and all will come right.]

Job maintains his righteousness

"[God] has torn me in his wrath and persecuted me.
He has gnashed on me with his teeth.
My adversary sharpens his eyes on me.
They have gaped on me with their mouth.
They have struck me on the cheek reproachfully.
They gather themselves together against me.
God delivers me to the ungodly,
and casts me into the hands of the wicked.
I was at ease, and he broke me apart.
Yes, he has taken me by the neck, and dashed me to pieces.
He has also set me up for his target.
His archers surround me.
He splits my kidneys apart, and does not spare.
He pours out my bile on the ground.
He breaks me with breach on breach.
He runs at me like a giant.
I have sewed sackcloth on my skin,
and have thrust my horn in the dust.
My face is red with weeping.
Deep darkness is on my eyelids.
Although there is no violence in my hands,
and my prayer is pure.'"

Job demands the right to confront God

"Even today my complaint is rebellious.
His hand is heavy in spite of my groaning.
Oh that I knew where I might find him!
That I might come even to his seat!
I would set my cause in order before him,
and fill my mouth with arguments.
I would know the words which he would answer me,
and understand what he would tell me.
Would he contend with me in the greatness of his power?
No, but he would listen to me.
There the upright might reason with him,
so I should be delivered forever from my judge.

If I go east, he is not there;
if west, I can't find him;
He works to the north, but I can't see him.
He turns south, but I can't catch a glimpse of him."

God appears to Job

Then Yahweh answered Job out of the whirlwind,
"Who is this who darkens counsel
by words without knowledge?
Brace yourself like a man,
for I will question you, then you answer me!

"Where were you when I laid the foundations of the earth?
Declare, if you have understanding.
Who determined its measures, if you know?
Or who stretched the line on it?
What were its foundations fastened on?
Or who laid its cornerstone,
when the morning stars sang together,
and all the sons of God shouted for joy?

"Or who shut up the sea with doors,
when it broke out of the womb,
when I made clouds its garment,
and wrapped it in thick darkness,
marked out for it my bound,
set bars and doors,
and said, 'You may come here, but no further.
Your proud waves shall be stopped here?'

"Have you commanded the morning in your days,
and caused the dawn to know its place,
that it might take hold of the ends of the earth,
and shake the wicked out of it?
It is changed as clay under the seal,
and presented as a garment.
From the wicked, their light is withheld.
The high arm is broken.

"Have you entered into the springs of the sea?
Or have you walked in the recesses of the deep?
Have the gates of death been revealed to you?
Or have you seen the gates of the shadow of death?
Have you comprehended the earth in its width?
Declare, if you know it all.

"What is the way to the dwelling of light?
As for darkness, where is its place,
that you should take it to its bound,
that you should discern the paths to its house?
Surely you know, for you were born then,
and the number of your days is great!
Have you entered the treasuries of the snow,
or have you seen the treasures of the hail,
which I have reserved against the time of trouble,
against the day of battle and war?
By what way is the lightning distributed,
or the east wind scattered on the earth?

"Who has cut a channel for the flood water,
or the path for the thunder storm,
to cause it to rain on a land where there is no man,
on the wilderness, in which there is no man,
to satisfy the waste and desolate ground,
to cause the tender grass to grow?
Does the rain have a father?
Or who fathers the drops of dew?
"Whose womb did the ice come out of?
Who has given birth to the gray frost of the sky?
The waters become hard like stone,
when the surface of the deep is frozen."

Job replies

Then Job answered Yahweh,
"I know that you can do all things,
and that no purpose of yours can be restrained.
You asked, 'Who is this who hides counsel without knowledge?'
therefore I have uttered that which I didn't understand,
things too wonderful for me, which I didn't know.
You said, 'Listen, now, and I will speak;
I will question you, and you will answer me.'
I had heard of you by the hearing of the ear,
but now my eye sees you.
Therefore I abhor myself,
and repent in dust and ashes."

Conclusion

Yahweh gave Job twice as much as he had before. Then came there to him all
his brothers, and all his sisters, and all those who had been of his acquaintance
before, and ate bread with him in his house. They comforted him, and
consoled him concerning all the evil that Yahweh had brought on him.
Everyone also gave him a piece of money, and everyone a ring of gold.

So Yahweh blessed the latter end of Job more than his beginning. He had
fourteen thousand sheep, six thousand camels, one thousand yoke of oxen,
and a thousand female donkeys. He had also seven sons and three daughters.
. . . In all the land were no women found so beautiful as the daughters of Job.
Their father gave them an inheritance among their brothers. After this Job
lived one hundred forty years, and saw his sons, and his sons' sons, to four
generations. So Job died, being old and full of days.

The Talmud

Translated by Joseph Barclay, (1878), at sacred-texts.com. Introduction by Tim Davis (2016).

The Talmud is an immense collection (sixty-three Tractates or some 6,200 pages) of the important texts of rabbinic Judaism assembled between 200 and 500 CE. With the destruction of the Temple in 70 CE (and no place to serve as the center of Jewish teaching and authority), the Talmud began to become an organized way of preserving tradition in the form of structured discussions, legal analysis, and points of view. Beginning in oral tradition, it is written in Jewish Babylonian Aramaic and a dialect of ancient biblical Hebrew. There are thus two versions of the Talmud which were produced in two different parts of the ancient Jewish world: the Babylonian Talmud and the Palestinian (or Jerusalem) Talmud. Not only do they contain ancient discussions of tradition, but borrowed Greek and Persian terms that over time became difficult to interpret as well. It therefore became necessary in the Middle Ages to produce commentaries (such as those by the Geonim Rashi, Hananel, Gershom) on the commentary (Talmud). These works became integral to ongoing Jewish scholarship. The Talmud is still very much used by Orthodox and Conservative traditions today.

In the Passover passage below, we will often see a debate among the rabbis concerning how Jews should practice their faith as interpreted in the Torah (the first five books), tradition, and other parts of the Tanak (canon of Hebrew scriptures).

Treatise III

CHAPTER VII
On the Sabbath

1. The Sages laid down a great rule for the Sabbath: "Everyone who forgets the principle of Sabbath, and did many works on many Sabbaths, is only responsible for one sin-offering. Everyone who knows the principle of Sabbath, and did many works on many Sabbaths, is responsible for every Sabbath. Everyone who knows that there is Sabbath, and did many works on many Sabbaths, is responsible for every principal work. Everyone who has done many works, springing from one principal work, is only responsible for one sin-offering."

2. The principal works are forty, less one--sowing, ploughing, reaping, binding sheaves, threshing, winnowing, sifting, grinding, riddling, kneading, baking, shearing wool, whitening, carding, dyeing, spinning,

warping, making two spools, weaving two threads, taking out two threads, twisting, loosing, sewing two stitches, tearing thread for two sewings, hunting the gazelle, slaughtering, skinning, salting, curing its skin, tanning, cutting up, writing two letters, erasing to write two letters, building, demolishing, quenching, kindling, hammering, carrying from private to public property. Lo, these are principal works--forty, less one.

TREATISE V

CHAPTER I

One the Day of Atonement

1. Seven says before the Day of Atonement the High Priest was removed from his house to the chamber Parhedrin, and the council prepared for him another priest, lest there happen to him any defilement. R. Judah said, "They prepared also another wife, lest his wife die; as is said, 'And he shall atone for himself and for his house (i.e., for his wife).'" The Sages said to him, "If so, there is no end to the matter."

2. All these seven days, he (the high priest) sprinkled the blood, burned the incense, and trimmed the lamps, and offered the head and the foot. On the remainder of all the days, if he wished to offer, he offered; since the high priest first offered part, and first took part (in the sacrifices).

3. The elders from the elders of the great Sanhedrin delivered to him, and read before him, the ceremonial of the day; and they said to him, "My Lord High Priest, read with thy mouth, perchance thou hast forgotten, or perchance thou hast not learned." On the eve of the day of atonement, towards dawn, they placed him in the eastern gate (of the Temple), and they caused to pass before him bullocks, rams, and lambs, that he might be skilled and expert in his ministry.

4. All the seven days they did not withhold from him food and drink; the eve of the day of atonement, with the beginning of darkness, they did not permit him to eat much, since food induces sleep.

5. The elders of the great Sanhedrin delivered him to the elders of the priesthood, who brought him to the upper chamber of the house Abtinas. And they administered to him the oath, and they left him and departed. And they. said to him, "My Lord High Priest, we are ambassadors of the great Sanhedrin, and thou art our ambassador, and the ambassador of

the great Sanhedrin. We adjure thee by Him, whose Name dwells in this house, that thou wilt not change aught of all which we have said to thee." He went apart and wept. They went apart and wept.

6. If he were a learned man, he expounded; but if not, the disciples of the learned expounded before him. If he were skilled in reading, he read; but if not, they read before him. "And in what did they read before him?" "In Job, and in Ezra, and in Chronicles." Zachariah, the son of Kebutal, said, "I often read before him in Daniel."

7. If he desired to sleep, the young priests filliped with the first finger before him, and said to him, "My Lord High Priest, stand up and refresh thyself once on the pavement," and they kept him occupied until the time approached for slaying (the victims).

8. Every day they cleansed the altar at cockcrow, or at its approach, intermediate before or after it; and on the day of atonement at midnight; and in the three great feasts, at the first watch. And before cockcrow the court was crowded with Israel.

pp. 119-120

TREATISE V

CHAPTER I

On the Passover

1. On the eve of the fourteenth day of Nisan men search for leaven by candlelight. Every place where men do not bring in leaven, there is no need of search. "And wherefore do they say, two lines of barrels in the wine cellar?" "The place is meant into which persons bring leaven," The school of Shammai say, "two rows in front of the whole cellar." But the school of Hillel say, "The two outer lines on the top."

2. People need not suspect, lest perchance the weasel have slipped (with leaven) from house to house or from place to place. If so, from court to court, from city to city, there is no end to the matter.

3. Rabbi Judah said, "Men search on the eve of the fourteenth and on the morning of the fourteenth day, and at the time of burning it." But the Sages say, "If one did not search on the eve of the fourteenth, he must search on the fourteenth; if he did not search on the fourteenth, he must

search during the feast; if he did not search during the feast, he must search after the feast; and whatever remains, he shall leave well concealed, that there be no further need of search after it."

4. Rabbi Meier said, "Men may eat it till five o'clock, and burn it at the beginning of six." Rabbi Judah said, "They may eat it till four, and they are in suspense about five, but they burn it at the beginning of six."

5. And again said R. Judah, "Two loaves of the disallowed praise-offering were placed on the portico of the Temple enclosure; whilst they were placed there, all the people might eat leaven. If one were taken down they were in suspense; they neither ate nor burned it. When both were taken down they began to burn it." Rabban Gamaliel said, "Men may eat ordinary food till four o'clock, and the heave-offering till five o'clock, but they burned the leaven at six o'clock.

Midrash

From *The Wisdom of Israel*, by Edwin Collins (1910), at sacred-texts.com. Introduction by Tim Davis (2016).

> *The* Midrash *are a collection of stories, sermons, and exegesis of the Torah, as well as both legal and non-legal commentaries from rabbinic literature. Their purpose is to seek, study, and inquire. Originally these teachings and discussions were preserved orally, but they began to be written down in the second century CE. At a time when the Hebrew canon of scriptures was being set (and new texts could not be added), the* Midrash *were a way of expanding the tradition, commenting upon it, and interpreting the fixed body of canonical revelation. It was also a way of preserving the wisdom of the rabbis in regard to the understanding of Jewish tradition. Some* Midrash *are included in the Talmud. Today, the* Midrash *function chiefly as homiletical or exegetical commentaries on the scriptures.*

THE GREEDY PRINCE: THE VINE IS NOT WATERED WITH WINE

God needs no sacrifice, but the sacrificial worship had, for one of its objects, the weaning of Israel from idolatry and temptation to the cruelty to animals practiced by idolaters in sacrificing to devils and the supposed powers of evil. Rabbi Phineas said, in the name of Rabbi Levi:

"This may be likened to a king's son, who was greedy and who used to eat at the tables of all kinds of people, and learned their ways, and used to eat unclean food. Then the king said, "He shall always eat at my table, and there he shall remain.""

Thus, because the children of Israel were yearning after the idolatry they had seen in Egypt, and "sacrificing unto devils," they were commanded to bring sacrifices to the God of life, and to Him alone; to kill only in a merciful manner, and not to shed the blood of animals at all without the solemnity of an offering.

But the heathen thought their gods required food, whereas even mortal man, when in close intercourse with God, requires neither eating nor drinking; for Moses was forty days in the mount without food. How much less can the Holy One of Israel be in need of the flesh of sacrifices! The idea is ridiculed in the Psalms. Rabbi Chiya bar Abba says: "Even the lowest of God's creatures are not in need of their own produce; how much less then is the Creator in need of what He has created. Have ye ever heard it said, 'Irrigate this vine with wine, so that it may produce much wine, or this olive-tree with oil, that it may produce much oil?' These plants are in no need of their own products to nourish them; shall, then, God be in need of what He has created?"

Vayikra Rabbah, Chap. XXII., and *Barmidbar Rabbah*, Chap. XXI. pp. 32-33

THE LAMP THAT GOES OUT WHEN ITS LIGHT IS DONE, AND THE FIGS THAT ARE GATHERED IN THEIR DUE SEASON

What is the difference between the death of the aged and the death of the young?

Rabbi Judah says:—"When a lamp goes out of itself, it is good for the lamp and good for the wick, for the lamp is not broken and the wick does not form coal; but when men extinguish it, it is bad for the lamp, and bad for the wick."

Rabbi Abahu said:—"When you pluck figs at their proper season, it is good for the figs, and good for the fig-tree. But if figs be gathered before their time, it is bad for the figs and bad for the fig-tree."

Then why do we often see the righteous die young?

A story told of Rabbi Chiya bar Aba and his disciples, and according to others of Rabbi Akiba and his disciples, and of Rabbi Joshuah, and also of Rabbi Josi ben Chalafta and his disciples, explains this, by a parable.

It was their custom to rise early in the morning, and to sit and teach under a certain fig-tree. And the owner of the fig-tree used to rise early and gather the figs. The scholars thought that they were suspected, and that the figs were gathered early lest the Rabbi and his disciples might eat some of them. What did they? They changed their place of meeting.

Then the owner of the fig-tree went after them, and when he found them he said:

"My masters, You were wont to confer a *Mitzvah* upon me. You used to show me honor, and give me a share in your reward for the study of God's word, and give me the privilege of contributing my share to your deeds of piety, by coming and studying under my fig-tree. Will you now rob me of this privilege, this honor, this religious duty; and so make void all your former kindness? Why have you changed your meeting place?"

Then they told him that they thought perhaps he suspected they might eat some of the figs, because he always rose so early in the morning to gather them.

"God forbid," exclaimed the owner of the fig-tree; "I rise early to gather the figs because, if the sun shines brightly upon them, they breed worms."

So he persuaded them to return and study under his fig-tree. That morning he did not gather the figs, and the sun shone on the fig-tree, and the ripe fruit bred worms, and was no longer fit to gather.

Then said the Rabbi and his students:

"The master of the fig-tree knows the season of each fig, and when it ought to be gathered, and gathers it. Thus the Holy One, blessed be He, knows the season of the righteous, and when it is best to remove them from this. world."

pp. 18-20

Jewish Prayers

PRAYER ON ENTERING THE SYNAGOGUE

From *The Standard Prayer Book*, tr. by Simeon Singer, (1915), at sacred-texts.com

On entering the Synagogue say the following:

As for me, in the abundance of thy loving kindness will I come into thy house: I will worship toward thy holy temple in the fear of thee.

Into the house of God we will walk with the throng.

How goodly are thy tents, O Jacob, thy dwelling places, O Israel! As for me, in the abundance of thy lovingkindness will I come into thy house: I will worship toward thy holy temple in the fear of thee. Lord, I love the habitation of thy house, and the place where thy glory dwelleth. As for me, I will worship and bow down: I will bend the knee before the Lord, my Maker. And as for me, may my prayer unto thee, O Lord, be in an acceptable time: O God, in the abundance of thy lovingkindness, answer me in the truth of thy salvation.

CONFESSION ON A DEATH-BED

I acknowledge unto thee, O Lord my God and God of my fathers, that both my cure and my death are in thy hands. May it be thy will to send me a perfect healing. Yet if my death be fully determined by thee, I will in love accept it at thy hand. O may my death be an atonement for all the sins, iniquities and transgressions of which I have been guilty against thee, vouchsafe unto me of the bounding happiness that is treasured up for the righteous. Make known to me the path of life: in thy presence is fullness of joy; at thy right hand are pleasures for evermore.

Thou who art the father of the fatherless and judge of the widow, protect my beloved kindred with whose soul my own is knit. Into thy hand I commend my spirit; thou hast redeemed me, O Lord God of truth, Amen, and Amen!

The Lord reigneth; the Lord hath reigned; the Lord shall reign for ever and ever. *(To be said three times.)*

Blessed be His name, whose glorious kingdom is for ever and ever. *(To be said three times.)*

The Lord he is God. *(To be said seven times.)*

Hear, O Israel: the Lord our God, the Lord is one.

Near Eastern Mythology

Enuma Elish

Excerpts from the Babylonian Creation Myth, *Enuma Elish*, from sacred-texts.com, translated by L.W. King, introduced and emended by Sue Burnam

Enuma Elish, which means "when on high," is a creation story from the second millennium BCE. Apsu and Tiamat were father and mother of heaven and earth -- the primordial parents of all. Apsu was associated with fresh water and Tiamat with salt sea water. The "mingling of the waters" resulted in many generations of gods and goddesses who were associated with natural phenomena. Enuma Elish recounts the conflict among the gods which results in the creation of the heavens, the earth, and human beings by the god Marduk.

In ancient Mesopotamia, though people worshipped many gods, each city-state would honor one god in particular among the many. Marduk's triumph over Tiamat earns him the city of Babylon as his seat and supremacy over the gods as his reward.

Creation of the gods

When on high heaven was not named,
And the earth beneath did not yet bear a name,
And the primeval Apsu, who begat them,
And chaos, Tiamat, the mother of them both
Their waters were mingled together,
And no field was formed, no marsh was to be seen;
When of the gods none had been called into being,
And none bore a name, and no destinies were ordained;
Then were created the gods in the midst of heaven,

[Many generations of gods then descend from the primordial pair, Apsu and Tiamat.]

War among the gods

But Tiamat and Apsu were still in confusion . . .
They were troubled and . . .
In disorder . . .
 [Apsu and his advisor propose a plan to destroy the younger gods so that
Apsu and Tiamat can get some rest]
"And unto Tiamat, the glistening one, [Apsu] addressed the word: . . .
By day I cannot rest, by night I cannot lie down in peace.
But I will destroy their way, I will . . .
Let there be lamentation, and let us lie down again in peace."
When Tiamat heard these words,
She raged and cried aloud . . .
She uttered a curse, and unto Apsu she spake:
"What then shall we do?
Let their way be made difficult, and let us lie down again in peace."
[The god Ea learns of the plan and kills Apsu before it can be carried out]

Tiamat goes to war against the younger gods to avenge the death of Apsu

They banded themselves together and at the side of Tiamat they advanced;
They were furious; they devised mischief without resting night and day.
They prepared for battle, fuming and raging;
They joined their forces and made war,
[Tiamat] who formed all things,
Made in addition weapons invincible; she spawned monster-serpents,
Sharp of tooth, and merciless of fang;
With poison, instead of blood, she filled their bodies.
Fierce monster-vipers she clothed with terror,
With splendor she decked them, she made them of lofty stature.
Whoever beheld them, terror overcame him,
Their bodies reared up and none could withstand their attack.

. . . .
Tiamat made weighty her handiwork,
Evil she wrought against the gods her children.
To avenge Apsu, Tiamat planned evil . . .

[Several gods lead forces against Tiamat and her monsters and are defeated.
Then the god Marduk, the god of Babylon, rises to the challenge.]

The gods agree to reward Marduk if he prevails against Tiamat

To set out against Tiamat [Marduk's] heart hath prompted him.
He opened his mouth and spoke unto me, saying:
'If I, your avenger,
Conquer Tiamat and give you life,
Appoint an assembly, make my fate preeminent and proclaim it.
In [the heavenly council] seat yourselves joyfully together;
With my word in place of you will I decree fate.
May whatsoever I do remain unaltered,
May the word of my lips never be changed nor made of no avail.'
Hasten, therefore, and swiftly decree for him the fate which you bestow,
That he may go and fight your strong enemy!

They prepared for him a lordly chamber,
Before his fathers as prince he took his place.
"Thou art chief among the great gods,
Thy fate is unequaled . . .
O Marduk, thou art chief among the great gods,
Thy fate is unequaled, thy word is Anu!
Henceforth not without avail shall be thy command,
In thy power shall it be to exalt and to abase.
Established shall be the word of thy mouth, irresistible shall be thy command,
None among the gods shall transgress thy boundary.
Abundance, the desire of the shrines of the gods,
Shall be established in thy sanctuary, even though they lack offerings.
O Marduk, thou art our avenger!
. . . .
"May thy fate, O lord, be supreme among the gods,
To destroy and to create; speak thou the word, and thy command shall be
fulfilled.
Command now and let the garment vanish;
And speak the word again and let the garment reappear!
Then he spoke with his mouth, and the garment vanished;
Again he commanded it, and. the garment reappeared.
When the gods, his fathers, beheld the fulfillment of his word,
They rejoiced, and they did homage unto him, saying, "Marduk is king!"
They bestowed upon him the scepter, and the throne, and the ring,
They give him an invincible weaponry which overwhelmeth the foe.

"Go, and cut off the life of Tiamat,
And let the wind carry her blood into secret places."
After the gods his fathers had decreed for the lord his fate,
They caused him to set out on a path of prosperity and success.
He made ready the bow, he chose his weapon,
He slung a spear upon him and fastened it . . .
He raised the club, in his right hand he grasped it,
The bow and the quiver he hung at his side.
He set the lightning in front of him,
With burning flame he filled his body.
He made a net to enclose the inward parts of Tiamat,
The four winds he stationed so that nothing of her might escape;
The South wind and the North wind and the East wind and the West wind
He brought near to the net, the gift of his father Anu. . . .
With overpowering brightness his head was crowned.
Then he set out, he took his way,
And toward the raging Tiamat he set his face.

Marduk challenges Tiamat

'Stand! I and thou, let us join battle!'
When Tiamat heard these words,
She was like one possessed, she lost her reason.
Tiamat uttered wild, piercing cries,
She trembled and shook to her very foundations.
She recited an incantation, she pronounced her spell,
And the gods of the battle cried out for their weapons.
Then advanced Tiamat and Marduk, the counselor of the gods;
To the fight they came on, to the battle they drew nigh.
The lord spread out his net and caught her,
And the evil wind that was behind him he let loose in her face.
As Tiamat opened her mouth to its full extent,
He drove in the evil wind, while as yet she had not shut her lips.
The terrible winds filled her belly,
And her courage was taken from her, and her mouth she opened wide.
He seized the spear and burst her belly,
He severed her inward parts, he pierced her heart.
He overcame her and cut off her life;

He cast down her body and stood upon it.
When he had slain Tiamat, the leader,
Her might was broken, her host was scattered.
And the gods her helpers, who marched by her side,
Trembled, and were afraid, and turned back.
They took to flight to save their lives . . .

And the lord stood upon Tiamat's hinder parts,
And with his merciless club he smashed her skull.
He cut through the channels of her blood,
And he made the North wind bear it away into secret places.
His fathers beheld, and they rejoiced and were glad;
Presents and gifts they brought unto him.

Marduk establishes the heavens and the earth

Then the lord rested, gazing upon her dead body,
[He] devised a cunning plan.
He split her up like a flat fish into two halves;
One half of her he stablished as a covering for heaven.
He fixed a bolt, he stationed a watchman,
And bade them not to let her waters come forth.
He passed through the heavens, he surveyed the regions thereof,
And over against the Deep he set the dwelling of Nudimmud.
And the lord measured the structure of the Deep,
And he founded E-sara, a mansion like unto it.
The mansion E-sara which he created as heaven,
He caused [the gods] in their districts to inhabit.
He (Marduk) made the stations for the great gods;
The stars, their images, as the stars of the Zodiac, he fixed.
He ordained the year and into sections he divided it;
For the twelve months he fixed three stars.
After he had . . . the days of the year . . . images,
He founded the station of [the planet Jupiter] to determine their bounds;
That none might err or go astray,
. . .

Marduk creates human beings

[Marduk said]
"My blood will I take and bone will I fashion. . .[1]

I will create man who shall inhabit the earth,
That the service of the gods may be established, and that their shrines may be built."

---

[1] Some texts have human beings created from the blood of Tiamat's ally Kingu, mixed with earth.

12

Christianity

Selections from the Letters of Paul

Introduction by Mark Bocija and Tim Davis.

The teachings of Jesus formed the foundation of a new religious movement. Of crucial importance to the future of Christianity was the career of Paul (or Saul) of Tarsus (c. 5 to c. 67 CE). He was the first to write and record in his letters what would later become part of the New Testament corpus of the Bible. While his ministry may have begun a bit earlier, his letters are now believed by scholars to have been composed between 50 and 57 CE. (Not all of the letters attributed to him are now believed to be by his hand.) The Synoptic Gospels (Mark, Matthew, and Luke), which began in an evolving oral tradition, were all written down some twenty to thirty years later, while John was written sometime in the late 90's CE. As Paul is the first to write, he has the huge advantage of establishing his point of view and defining for countless followers how they would interpret the life and message of Jesus. (While Paul was a contemporary of Jesus, it is almost certain the apostle never met him during Jesus's earthly life. However, Paul claims in the letter below that the risen Christ did appear to him.) In the years following the crucifixion, the Jesus movement was transformed from an obscure Jewish sect to a group whose message of salvation was preached to the Gentiles as well as the Jews. The assertion that Christ's death and resurrection redeemed the believer and rescued him or her from death was not expressed by all Christians in the first century. One of the most influential of all Christian theologians, Paul began the task of interpreting the life and teaching of Jesus and thus began the creation of a body of theological doctrine. In the selections below are two of the most significant passages from Paul's writings. The first is from the Letter to the Corinthians in which Paul defends the redeeming power of Christ's death and resurrection. It was likely dictated by Paul to his secretary between 53 and 54 CE. The second is from the Letter to the Romans, dating around 57 CE, in which Paul lays the foundation for the doctrine of original sin and salvation by faith alone.

Now I am reminding you, brothers, of the gospel I preached to you, which you indeed received and in which you also stand. Through it you are also being saved, if you hold fast to the word I preached to you, unless you believed in vain. For I handed on to you as of first importance what I also received: that Christ died for our sins in accordance with the scriptures; that he was buried; that he was raised on the third day in accordance with the scriptures; that he appeared to Kephas, then to the Twelve.

After that, he appeared to more than five hundred brothers at once, most of whom are still living, though some have fallen asleep. After that he appeared to James, then to all the apostles.

Last of all, as to one born abnormally, he appeared to me.

For I am the least of the apostles, not fit to be called an apostle, because I persecuted the church of God. But by the grace of God I am what I am, and his grace to me has not been ineffective. Indeed, I have toiled harder than all of them; not I, however, but the grace of God (that is) with me. Therefore, whether it be I or they, so we preach and so you believed. But if Christ is preached as raised from the dead, how can some among you say there is no resurrection of the dead?

If there is no resurrection of the dead, then neither has Christ been raised. And if Christ has not been raised, then empty (too) is our preaching; empty, too, your faith.

Then we are also false witnesses to God, because we testified against God that he raised Christ, whom he did not raise if in fact the dead are not raised. For if the dead are not raised, neither has Christ been raised, and if Christ has not been raised, your faith is vain; you are still in your sins. Then those who have fallen asleep in Christ have perished.

If for this life only we have hoped in Christ, we are the most pitiable people of all. But now Christ has been raised from the dead, the first-fruits of those who have fallen asleep. For since death came through a human being, the resurrection of the dead came also through a human being. For just as in Adam all die, so too in Christ shall all be brought to life, but each one in proper order: Christ the first fruits; then, at his coming, those who belong to Christ; then comes the end, when he hands over the kingdom to his God and Father, when he has destroyed every sovereignty and every authority and power.

For he must reign until he has put all his enemies under his feet. The last enemy to be destroyed is death, for "he subjected everything under his feet." But when it says that everything has been subjected, it is clear that it excludes the one who subjected everything to him. When everything is subjected to him, then the Son himself will (also) be subjected to the one who subjected everything to him, so that God may be all in all.

Otherwise, what will people accomplish by having themselves baptized for the dead? If the dead are not raised at all, then why are they having themselves baptized for them?

Moreover, why are we endangering ourselves all the time?

Every day I face death; I swear it by the pride in you (brothers) that I have in Christ Jesus our Lord. If at Ephesus I fought with beasts, so to speak, what benefit was it to me? If the dead are not raised: "Let us eat and drink, for tomorrow we die." Do not be led astray: "Bad company corrupts good morals." Become sober as you ought and stop sinning. For some have no knowledge of God; I say this to your shame. But someone may say, "How are the dead raised? With what kind of body will they come back?" You fool! What you sow is not brought to life unless it dies. And what you sow is not the body that is to be but a bare kernel of wheat, perhaps, or of some other kind; but God gives it a body as he chooses, and to each of the seeds its own body.

Letter to the Romans 3
God's Faithfulness

[1]What advantage, then, is there in being a Jew, or what value is there in circumcision? [2]Much in every way! First of all, they have been entrusted with the very words of God. [3]What if some did not have faith? Will their lack of faith nullify God's faithfulness? [4]Not at all! Let God be true, and every man a liar. As it is written: "So that you may be proved right when you speak and prevail when you judge." [5]But if our unrighteousness brings out God's righteousness more clearly, what shall we say? That God is unjust in bringing his wrath on us? (I am using a human argument.) [6]Certainly not! If that were so, how could God judge the world? [7]Someone might argue, "If my falsehood enhances God's truthfulness and so increases his glory, why am I still condemned as a sinner?" [8]Why not say—as we are being slanderously reported as saying and as some claim that we say—"Let us do evil that good may result?" Their condemnation is deserved.

1. No One is Righteous

[9]What shall we conclude then? Are we any better? Not at all! We have already made the charge that Jews and Gentiles alike are all under sin. [10]As it is written: "There is no one righteous, not even one; [11]there is no one who understands, no one who seeks God. [12]All have turned away, they have together become worthless; there is no one who does good, not even one." [13]"Their throats are open graves; their tongues practice deceit. The poison of vipers is on their lips.

[14]"Their mouths are full of cursing and bitterness [15]Their feet are swift to shed blood; [16]ruin and misery mark their ways, [17]and the way of peace they do not know. [18]There is no fear of God before their eyes." [19]Now we know that whatever the law says, it says to those who are under the law, so that every mouth may be silenced and the whole world held accountable to God. [20]Therefore no one will be declared righteous in his sight by observing the law; rather, through the law we become conscious of sin.

Righteousness Through Faith

[21]But now a righteousness from God, apart from law, has been made known, to which the Law and the Prophets testify. [22]This righteousness from God comes through faith in Jesus Christ to all who believe. There is no difference, [23]for all have sinned and fall short of the glory of God, [24]and are justified freely by his grace through the redemption that came by Christ Jesus. [25]God presented him as a sacrifice of atonement, through faith in his blood. He did this to demonstrate his justice, because in his forbearance he had left the sins committed beforehand unpunished— [26]he did it to demonstrate his justice at the present time, so as to be just and the one who justifies those who have faith in Jesus. [27]Where, then, is boasting? It is excluded. On what principle? On that of observing the law? No, but on that of faith. [28]For we maintain that a man is justified by faith apart from observing the law. [29]Is God the God of Jews only? Is he not the God of Gentiles too? Yes, of Gentiles too, [30]since there is only one God, who will justify the circumcised by faith and the uncircumcised through that same faith. [31]Do we, then, nullify the law by this faith? Not at all! Rather, we uphold the law.

Selections From The Gospel Of Matthew

Introduction by Tim Davis and Mark Bocija.

Historical and critical scholars of the New Testament now believe that the Gospel of Matthew was written (in Greek) sometime after the year 80 for a Christian community within the Jewish homeland. We do not specifically know who the author was. Likely, the evangelist was a Jewish-Christian male caught up in the struggle to establish the message of Jesus in a Roman-occupied Jewish society. The gospel later gets attributed by second-century Church Fathers (such as Papias) to the tradition of the apostle Matthew. The entire gospel is a reflection of the growing tension between traditional Jewish values and those of the Jewish Christians struggling to make sense of the life and ministry of the historical Jesus. Christians took up this struggle amid the tensions of a Roman-occupied Judea. The passage below speaks to some of these issues and the evolving values of those Jews who found an appeal in the Christian movement that for all intents and purposes was still a part of Judaism in the Jewish homeland.

The idea of a radical and universal equality based on faith alone was a remarkable feature of Jesus's teaching that contrasts sharply with the religious traditions of the ancient world. Religious traditions of the Roman world were not universal; they included some people and not others. The state religion, the worship of the Roman gods, was for the benefit of citizens and for the preservation of the Empire, not its enemies. People who were not citizens of the empire would not worship Roman gods. Mystery religions, although popular across the empire and even beyond, were restricted to certain populations. The cult of Mithra, for example, began as a cult restricted to soldiers and never permitted women to join. Other cults were only for women. As the following miracle narratives from the Gospel of Matthew demonstrate, the benefits of faith in Jesus are not restricted to an individual based on gender, ethnicity, citizenship, or even intellect. To illustrate the principal of equality in Christ, the evangelist has chosen two of the most disliked characters in Judea: a Canaanite and a Roman officer.

On a Universal Family Based in Faith
Matthew 15

Then Jesus went from that place and withdrew to the region of Tyre and Sidon.

22And behold, a Canaanite woman of that district came and called out, "Have pity on me, Lord, Son of David! My daughter is tormented by a demon."

²³But he did not say a word in answer to her. His disciples came and asked him, "Send her away, for she keeps calling out after us."

²⁴He said in reply, "I was sent only to the lost sheep of the house of Israel."

²⁵But the woman came and did him homage, saying, "Lord, help me."

²⁶He said in reply, "It is not right to take the food of the children and throw it to the dogs."

²⁷She said, "Please, Lord, for even the dogs eat the scraps that fall from the table of their masters."

²⁸Then Jesus said to her in reply, "O woman, great is your faith! Let it be done for you as you wish."

And her daughter was healed from that hour.

Matthew 8

⁴When he entered Capernaum, ⁵a centurion approached him and appealed to him,

⁶saying, "Lord, my servant is lying at home paralyzed, suffering dreadfully."

⁷He said to him, "I will come and cure him."

⁸The centurion said in reply, "Lord, I am not worthy to have you enter under my roof; only say the word and my servant will be healed.

⁹For I too am a person subject to authority, with soldiers subject to me. And I say to one, 'Go,' and he goes; and to another, 'Come here,' and he comes; and to my slave, 'Do this,' and he does it."

¹⁰When Jesus heard this, he was amazed and said to those following him, "Amen, I say to you, in no one in Israel have I found such faith.

¹¹I say to you, many will come from the east and the west, and will recline with Abraham, Isaac, and Jacob at the banquet in the kingdom of heaven, ¹²but the children of the kingdom will be driven out into the outer darkness, where there will be wailing and grinding of teeth."

¹³And Jesus said to the centurion, "You may go; as you have believed, let it be done for you." And at that very hour (his) servant was healed.

On Separation of Church and State
Matthew 12

In the following selection, Jesus rejects the almost universally held idea that the state is an extension of divine cosmic order. In Mesopotamia, the kings were the chosen ones of the gods. In Egypt, they were the incarnation of Ra. In the Greek and Roman traditions, the gods are the guardians of the state and piety to the gods is necessary for its survival.

[13]They sent some Pharisees and Herodians to him to ensnare him in his speech.

[14]They came and said to him, "Teacher, we know that you are a truthful man and that you are not concerned with anyone's opinion. You do not regard a person's status but teach the way of God in accordance with the truth. Is it lawful to pay the census tax to Caesar or not? Should we pay or should we not pay?"

[15]Knowing their hypocrisy he said to them, "Why are you testing me? Bring me a denarius to look at."

[16]They brought one to him and he said to them, "Whose image and inscription is this?" They replied to him, "Caesar's."

[17]So Jesus said to them, "Repay to Caesar what belongs to Caesar and to God what belongs to God." They were utterly amazed at him.

It is important to understand here that they are indeed asking him a legal question. For Jews, the Law of Moses contained in the Torah, (the first five books of the Hebrew scriptures or Old Testament) was the foundation for both the Jewish religion and the Jewish state. There should be no discrepancy between religious law and civil law. For this reason, many first-century Jews held that it was impossible to live according to God's law as long as Roman law superseded it. The question they are asking was a burning one at the time. Is it lawful according to Mosaic law, to pay the tax. They expected a legalistic answer supported by references to the Torah. What they got was something very different.

Sermon on the Mount

World English Bible
Matthew, Chapter 5

[1]Seeing the multitudes, he went up onto the mountain. When he had sat down, his disciples came to him. [2]He opened his mouth and taught them, saying,

[3]"Blessed are the poor in spirit, for theirs is the Kingdom of Heaven.

[4]Blessed are those who mourn, for they shall be comforted.

[5]Blessed are the gentle, for they shall inherit the earth.

[6]Blessed are those who hunger and thirst after righteousness, for they shall be filled.

[7]Blessed are the merciful, for they shall obtain mercy.

[8]Blessed are the pure in heart, for they shall see God.

[9]Blessed are the peacemakers, for they shall be called children of God.

[10]Blessed are those who have been persecuted for righteousness' sake, for theirs is the Kingdom of Heaven.

[11]"Blessed are you when people reproach you, persecute you, and say all kinds of evil against you falsely, for my sake. [12]Rejoice, and be exceedingly glad, for great is your reward in heaven. For that is how they persecuted the prophets who were before you.

[13]"You are the salt of the earth, but if the salt has lost its flavor, with what will it be salted? It is then good for nothing, but to be cast out and trodden under the feet of men. [14]You are the light of the world. A city located on a hill can't be hidden. [15]Neither do you light a lamp, and put it under a measuring basket, but on a stand; and it shines to all who are in the house. [16]Even so, let your light shine before men; that they may see your good works, and glorify your Father who is in heaven.

[17]"Don't think that I came to destroy the law or the prophets. I didn't come to destroy, but to fulfill. [18]For most certainly, I tell you, until heaven and earth pass away, not even one smallest letter or one tiny pen stroke shall in any way pass away from the law, until all things are accomplished. [19]Whoever, therefore, shall break one of these least commandments, and teach others to do

so, shall be called least in the Kingdom of Heaven; but whoever shall do and teach them shall be called great in the Kingdom of Heaven. [20]For I tell you that unless your righteousness exceeds that of the scribes and Pharisees, there is no way you will enter into the Kingdom of Heaven. [21]"You have heard that it was said to the ancient ones, 'You shall not murder;' and 'Whoever murders will be in danger of the judgment.' [22]But I tell you that everyone who is angry with his brother without a cause will be in danger of the judgment. Whoever says to his brother, 'Raca!' will be in danger of the council. Whoever says, 'You fool!' will be in danger of the fire of Gehenna.

[23]"If therefore you are offering your gift at the altar, and there remember that your brother has anything against you, [24]leave your gift there before the altar, and go your way. First be reconciled to your brother, and then come and offer your gift. [25]Agree with your adversary quickly, while you are with him on the way; lest perhaps the prosecutor deliver you to the judge, and the judge deliver you to the officer, and you be cast into prison. [26]Most certainly I tell you, you shall by no means get out of there, until you have paid the last penny. [27]"You have heard that it was said, 'You shall not commit adultery;' [28]but I tell you that everyone who gazes at a woman to lust after her has committed adultery with her already in his heart. [29]If your right eye causes you to stumble, pluck it out and throw it away from you. For it is more profitable for you that one of your members should perish, than for your whole body to be cast into Gehenna. [30]If your right hand causes you to stumble, cut it off, and throw it away from you. For it is more profitable for you that one of your members should perish, than for your whole body to be cast into Gehenna. [31]"It was also said, 'Whoever shall put away his wife, let him give her a writing of divorce,' [32]but I tell you that whoever puts away his wife, except for the cause of sexual immorality, makes her an adulteress; and whoever marries her when she is put away commits adultery.

[33]"Again you have heard that it was said to the ancient ones, 'You shall not make false vows, but shall perform to the Lord your vows,' [34]but I tell you, don't swear at all: neither by heaven, for it is the throne of God; [35]nor by the earth, for it is the footstool of his feet; nor by Jerusalem, for it is the city of the great King. [36]Neither shall you swear by your head, for you can't make one hair white or black. [37]But let your 'Yes' be 'Yes' and your 'No' be 'No.' Whatever is more than these is of the evil one. [38]"You have heard that it was said, 'An eye for an eye, and a tooth for a tooth.' [39]But I tell you, don't resist him who is evil; but whoever strikes you on your right cheek, turn to him

the other also. [40]If anyone sues you to take away your coat, let him have your cloak also. [41]Whoever compels you to go one mile, go with him two. [42]Give to him who asks you, and don't turn away him who desires to borrow from you. [43]"You have heard that it was said, 'You shall love your neighbor and hate your enemy.' [44] ut I tell you, love your enemies, bless those who curse you, do good to those who hate you, and pray for those who mistreat you and persecute you, [45]that you may be children of your Father who is in heaven. For he makes his sun to rise on the evil and the good, and sends rain on the just and the unjust. [46]For if you love those who love you, what reward do you have? Don't even the tax collectors do the same? [47]If you only greet your friends, what more do you do than others? Don't even the tax collectors do the same? [48]Therefore you shall be perfect, just as your Father in heaven is perfect.

Matthew, Chapter 6

[1]"Be careful that you don't do your charitable giving before men, to be seen by them, or else you have no reward from your Father who is in heaven. [2]Therefore when you do merciful deeds, don't sound a trumpet before yourself, as the hypocrites do in the synagogues and in the streets, that they may get glory from men. Most certainly I tell you, they have received their reward. [3]But when you do merciful deeds, don't let your left hand know what your right hand does, [4]so that your merciful deeds may be in secret, then your Father who sees in secret will reward you openly.

[5]"When you pray, you shall not be as the hypocrites, for they love to stand and pray in the synagogues and in the corners of the streets, that they may be seen by men. Most certainly, I tell you, they have received their reward. [6]But you, when you pray, enter into your inner room, and having shut your door, pray to your Father who is in secret, and your Father who sees in secret will reward you openly. [7]In praying, don't use vain repetitions, as the Gentiles do; for they think that they will be heard for their much speaking. [8]Therefore don't be like them, for your Father knows what things you need, before you ask him. [9]Pray like this: 'Our Father in heaven, may your name be kept holy. [10]Let your Kingdom come. Let your will be done on earth as it is in heaven. [11]Give us today our daily bread. [12]Forgive us our debts, as we also forgive our debtors. [13]Bring us not into temptation, but deliver us from the evil one. For yours is the Kingdom, the power, and the glory forever. Amen.'

[14]"For if you forgive men their trespasses, your heavenly Father will also forgive you.

¹⁵But if you don't forgive men their trespasses, neither will your Father forgive your trespasses.

¹⁶"Moreover when you fast, don't be like the hypocrites, with sad faces. For they disfigure their faces, that they may be seen by men to be fasting. Most certainly I tell you, they have received their reward. ¹⁷But you, when you fast, anoint your head, and wash your face; ¹⁸so that you are not seen by men to be fasting, but by your Father who is in secret, and your Father, who sees in secret, will reward you.

¹⁹"Don't lay up treasures for yourselves on the earth, where moth and rust consume, and where thieves break through and steal; ²⁰but lay up for yourselves treasures in heaven, where neither moth nor rust consume, and where thieves don't break through and steal; ²¹for where your treasure is, there your heart will be also.

²²"The lamp of the body is the eye. If therefore your eye is sound, your whole body will be full of light. ²³But if your eye is evil, your whole body will be full of darkness. If therefore the light that is in you is darkness, how great is the darkness!

²⁴"No one can serve two masters, for either he will hate the one and love the other; or else he will be devoted to one and despise the other. You can't serve both God and Mammon. ²⁵Therefore I tell you, don't be anxious for your life: what you will eat, or what you will drink; nor yet for your body, what you will wear. Isn't life more than food, and the body more than clothing? ²⁶See the birds of the sky, that they don't sow, neither do they reap, nor gather into barns. Your heavenly Father feeds them. Aren't you of much more value than they? ²⁷"Which of you, by being anxious, can add one moment‡ to his lifespan? ²⁸Why are you anxious about clothing? Consider the lilies of the field, how they grow. They don't toil, neither do they spin, ²⁹yet I tell you that even Solomon in all his glory was not dressed like one of these. ³⁰But if God so clothes the grass of the field, which today exists, and tomorrow is thrown into the oven, won't he much more clothe you, you of little faith?

³¹"Therefore don't be anxious, saying, 'What will we eat?,' 'What will we drink?' or, 'With what will we be clothed?' ³²For the Gentiles seek after all these things; for your heavenly Father knows that you need all these things. ³³But seek first God's Kingdom, and his righteousness; and all these things will be given to you as well. ³⁴Therefore don't be anxious for tomorrow, for tomorrow will be anxious for itself. Each day's own evil is sufficient.

[1]"Don't judge, so that you won't be judged. [2]For with whatever judgment you judge, you will be judged; and with whatever measure you measure, it will be measured to you. [3]Why do you see the speck that is in your brother's eye, but don't consider the beam that is in your own eye? [4]Or how will you tell your brother, 'Let me remove the speck from your eye;' and behold, the beam is in your own eye? [5]You hypocrite! First remove the beam out of your own eye, and then you can see clearly to remove the speck out of your brother's eye.

[6]"Don't give that which is holy to the dogs, neither throw your pearls before the pigs, lest perhaps they trample them under their feet, and turn and tear you to pieces.

[7]"Ask, and it will be given you. Seek, and you will find. Knock, and it will be opened for you. [8]For everyone who asks receives. He who seeks finds. To him who knocks it will be opened. [9]Or who is there among you, who, if his son asks him for bread, will give him a stone? [10]Or if he asks for a fish, who will give him a serpent? [11] If you then, being evil, know how to give good gifts to your children, how much more will your Father who is in heaven give good things to those who ask him! [12]Therefore whatever you desire for men to do to you, you shall also do to them; for this is the law and the prophets.

[13]"Enter in by the narrow gate; for wide is the gate and broad is the way that leads to destruction, and many are those who enter in by it. [14]How narrow is the gate, and restricted is the way that leads to life! Few are those who find it.

[15]"Beware of false prophets, who come to you in sheep's clothing, but inwardly are ravening wolves. [16]By their fruits you will know them. Do you gather grapes from thorns, or figs from thistles? [17]Even so, every good tree produces good fruit; but the corrupt tree produces evil fruit. [18]A good tree can't produce evil fruit, neither can a corrupt tree produce good fruit. [19]Every tree that doesn't grow good fruit is cut down, and thrown into the fire. [20]Therefore by their fruits you will know them. [21]Not everyone who says to me, 'Lord, Lord,' will enter into the Kingdom of Heaven; but he who does the will of my Father who is in heaven. [22]Many will tell me in that day, 'Lord, Lord, didn't we prophesy in your name, in your name cast out demons, and in your name do many mighty works?' [23]Then I will tell them, 'I never knew you. Depart from me, you who work iniquity.'

[24]"Everyone therefore who hears these words of mine, and does them, I will

liken him to a wise man, who built his house on a rock. [25]The rain came down, the floods came, and the winds blew, and beat on that house; and it didn't fall, for it was founded on the rock. [26]Everyone who hears these words of mine, and doesn't do them will be like a foolish man, who built his house on the sand. [27]The rain came down, the floods came, and the winds blew, and beat on that house; and it fell—and great was its fall."

[28]When Jesus had finished saying these things, the multitudes were astonished at his teaching, [29]for he taught them with authority, and not like the scribes.

The Gospel of Luke

The Parable of the Good Samaritan
Luke, Chapter 10

[25]Behold, a certain lawyer stood up and tested him, saying, "Teacher, what shall I do to inherit eternal life?"

[26]He said to him, "What is written in the law? How do you read it?"

[27]He answered, "You shall love the Lord your God with all your heart, with all your soul, with all your strength, and with all your mind; and your neighbor as yourself."

[28]He said to him, "You have answered correctly. Do this, and you will live."

[29]But he, desiring to justify himself, asked Jesus, "Who is my neighbor?"

[30]Jesus answered, "A certain man was going down from Jerusalem to Jericho, and he fell among robbers, who both stripped him and beat him, and departed, leaving him half dead. [31]By chance a certain priest was going down that way. When he saw him, he passed by on the other side. [32]In the same way a Levite also, when he came to the place, and saw him, passed by on the other side. [33]But a certain Samaritan, as he traveled, came where he was. When he saw him, he was moved with compassion, [34]came to him, and bound up his wounds, pouring on oil and wine. He set him on his own animal, brought him to an inn, and took care of him. [35]On the next day, when he departed, he took out two denarii, gave them to the host, and said to him, 'Take care of him. Whatever you spend beyond that, I will repay you when I return.' [36]Now

which of these three do you think seemed to be a neighbor to him who fell among the robbers?"

[37]He said, "He who showed mercy on him." Then Jesus said to him, "Go and do likewise."

The Apocrypha

The Gospel of Thomas

Translations from the Oxyrhynchus Papyri by Thomas O. Lambdin, B.P Grenfell and A.S. Hunt (1887). Introduction by (Tim Davis 2016).

> *The Gospel of Thomas was composed from the tradition of the sayings of Jesus (possibly emanating from the region around Syria). The sayings were written down in Greek, maybe even as early as 120 CE, and appeared later in Egyptian Coptic texts. A copy of the Egyptian version of the gospel from the mid-300's has fully survived in the Nag Hammadi collection of documents. The Gospel of Thomas is an assemblage of some 114 sayings and attributions that a number of scholars believe are reflective of Gnostic Christian philosophies. About half of the Gospel of Thomas is paralleled in the Canonical Gospels of Matthew, Mark, Luke and John.*

These are the secret sayings which the living Jesus spoke and which Didymos Judas Thomas wrote down.

1. And He said, "Whoever finds the interpretation of these sayings will not experience death."

2. Jesus said, "Let him who seeks continue seeking until he finds.
   When he finds, he will become troubled.
   When he becomes troubled, he will be astonished, and he will rule over the All."

3. Jesus said, "If those who lead you say, 'See, the Kingdom is in the sky,' then the birds of the sky will precede you. If they say to you, 'It is in the sea,' then the fish will precede you.
   Rather, the Kingdom is inside of you, and it is outside of you. When you come to know yourselves, then you will become known, and you will realize that it is you who are the sons of the living Father. But if you will not know yourselves, you dwell in poverty and it is you who are that poverty."

4. Jesus said, "The man old in days will not hesitate to ask a small child seven days old about the place of life, and he will live. For many who are first will become last, and they will become one and the same."

5. Jesus said, "Recognize what is in your sight, and that which is hidden from you will become plain to you. For there is nothing hidden which will not become manifest."

6. His disciples questioned Him and said to Him, "Do you want us to fast? How shall we pray? Shall we give alms? What diet shall we observe?" Jesus said, "Do not tell lies, and do not do what you hate, for all things are plain in the sight of Heaven. For nothing hidden will not become manifest, and nothing covered will remain without being uncovered."

....

23. Jesus said, "I shall choose you, one out of a thousand, and two out of ten thousand, and they shall stand as a single one."

24. His disciples said to Him, "Show us the place where You are, since it is necessary for us to seek it."
He said to them, "Whoever has ears, let him hear. There is light within a man of light, and he (or "it") lights up the whole world. If he (or "it") does not shine, he (or "it") is darkness."

25. Jesus said, "Love your brother like your soul, guard him like the pupil of your eye."

....

37. His disciples said, "When will You become revealed to us and when shall we see You?" Jesus said, "When you disrobe without being ashamed and take up your garments and place them under your feet like little children and tread on them, then [will you see] the Son of the Living One, and you will not be afraid."

38. Jesus said, "Many times have you desired to hear these words which I am saying to you, and you have no one else to hear them from. There will be days when you look for Me and will not find Me."

39. Jesus said, "The Pharisees and the scribes have taken the keys of Knowledge and hidden them. They themselves have not entered, nor have they allowed to enter those who wish to. You, however, be as wise as serpents and as innocent as doves."

108. Jesus said, "He who will drink from my mouth will become like Me. I myself shall become he, and the things that are hidden will become revealed to him."

109. Jesus said, "The Kingdom is like a man who had a [hidden] treasure in his field without knowing it. And [after] he died, he left it to his son. The son did not know (about the treasure). He inherited the field and sold [it]. And the one who bought it went plowing and found the treasure. He began to lend money at interest to whomever he wished."

110. Jesus said, "Whoever finds the world and becomes rich, let him renounce the world."

111. Jesus said, "The heavens and the earth will be rolled up in your presence.
And one who lives from the Living One will not see death.
Does not Jesus say, 'Whoever finds himself is superior to the world?'"

112. Jesus said, "Woe to the flesh that depends on the soul; woe to the soul that depends on the flesh."

113. His disciples said to Him, "When will the Kingdom come?"
Jesus said, "It will not come by waiting for it.
It will not be a matter of saying 'Here it is' or 'There it is.'
Rather, the Kingdom of the Father is spread out upon the earth, and men do not see it."

114. Simon Peter said to Him, "Let Mary leave us, for women are not worthy of Life."
Jesus said, "I myself shall lead her in order to make her male, so that she too may become a living spirit resembling you males.
For every woman who will make herself male will enter the Kingdom of Heaven."

Tertullian

Prescription Against Heretics

Translated by Mark S. Bocija

(The section begins with Tertullian arguing against a variety of philosophical positions that he believes have distorted the truths of the faith.)

These false doctrines (the various philosophical schools) are created by men and demons for the satisfaction of itching ears[10], they are the product of what men currently call "wisdom. . . . " Philosophy may be the fabric and foundation of the wisdom of this world, but it is a reckless interpreter of the nature and disposition of the divine.[11]

Indeed, heresies themselves are spun out of philosophy. From philosophy comes concepts like *aeons*[12], countless numbers of forms (Platonic), and the doctrine of the trinity of man from the Platonist Valentinus. From philosophy also stems Marcion's god, superior in tranquility to our God, he came to us from the Stoics. Epicurus maintained that the soul dies, while all of the philosophical schools deny the resurrection of the body. Wherever men claim that matter is the same as God, you will find the teaching of Zeno, and wherever someone is postulating that God is fire, Heraclitus comes into it.

The same arguments are dragged out over and over again and the same issues are discussed by the heretics and philosophers: Where does evil come from and why does it exist? What is the origin of humanity and how did it come about? Then there is that question that Valentinus recently proposed: Where does God come from?

---

10 Obviously not literally itching ears. He is referring to those scholars who never satisfied with an explanation and always want to hear novel ideas.

11 In other words, while philosophy helps us to understand worldly things, it is not useful in helping us understand God.

12 Gnostic Christians held that there could be no direct interface between the eternal Being and the world of matter. The eternal being emanated a series of aeons or subordinate heavenly powers, each less perfect than the previous and further removed from the supreme deity. The least perfect emanation would serve as the connecting link between a perfect divinity and the material world and all its evils. Ideologies like this arose in response to the desire to reconcile philosophical notions of an utterly transcendent God with the Christian insistence that God interacts with humanity.

Poor Aristotle, who invented for them the dialectical method, that art of building up theories and tearing them down again, with its ever-changing conclusions, its forced conjectures, its harsh arguments, laborious in its contentions, burdensome even to itself, arguing against everything and, on the whole, explaining nothing.

This is the source of those fables and endless genealogies and fruitless questions and discourses that creep[13] like a cancer. The apostle Paul discouraged us from these things, and warned us specifically about philosophy and its empty seductions, as something we ought to guard against when he wrote to the Corinthians: "Do not allow anyone to entice you through philosophy and vain seductions so that you follow the traditions of men, and turn away from the wisdom of the Holy Spirit."

What indeed has Athens to do with Jerusalem? What common ground is there between the Academy[14] and the Church, between heretics and Christians? Our method of instruction comes from the porch of Solomon, who taught that the Lord must be sought in the simplicity of the heart.

Let those who propose a Stoic or Platonic or dialectical Christianity open their eyes. For us, there is no need of curious argumentation once we know Jesus Christ, no need of constant investigation after the Gospels. Since we believe, we desire nothing greater than to believe.

---

13   Literally, the word used here is "serpent" (Latin, *serpo*), creeping silently or slithering like a snake. The word play here is meant to reinforce the connection between the Satan, the serpent that misleads Adam and Eve in the Garden of Eden, and the discourses of the philosophers that also creep like serpents and mislead the faithful.

14   Plato's school was founded in 387 BCE. After his death, the Academy continued to flourished for over 900 years until 529 CE when it was closed by Emperor Justinian, who viewed it as a remnant of lingering paganism. It was still in operation when Tertullian was alive.

Clement of Alexandria

Stromata

Chapter XIX.-That the Philosophers Have Attained to Some Portion of Truth.

Many people have testified that the Greeks have established a great number of true opinions. Even Paul, in the Acts of the Apostles, is recorded to have said to the Areopagites;[15]

"I see that in every way you are religious men. For as I walked about and observed your religious objects, I noticed an altar with the inscription that reads, 'To an Unknown God.' I will tell you about this God whom you unknowingly worship. He has created the world and all things in it, since He is Lord of both heaven and earth, he does not dwell in temples made by human hands,[16] for he needs nothing from us. He is the one who gives life and breath to all things; He has made all nations of men. . . . He has determined the appointed time for everything, and the places where all should live. He did this so that mankind might seek God and reach out and find Him; even some of your own poets have said, For we also are His offspring."[17]

Since the apostle Paul himself made use of poetical examples from the Phenomena of Aratus, it is evident that he approved of what had been articulated by the Greeks. Furthermore, he implies that the Greeks by worshipping this "unknown God" were actually in an indirect way worshipping the Creator; but it was necessary for them to have a more direct knowledge of God and to apprehend Him and come to know Him through the Son. . . .

Naturally we do not accept absolutely all philosophy, but we do affirm that of which Socrates speaks in Plato:

"'And whom', said he, 'do you call the true philosophers?'

---

15   Members of a high Greek council.

16   Take this to mean that God does not require ritual sacrifices such as animal offerings

17   Paul is quoting Aratus (c. 315 - before 240 BC), who produced an enormously popular poem known as the Phenomena. While the bulk of the book is comprised of descriptions of the constellations, it is peppered with mythological and literary allusions. The literary content was the basis of its popularity not the astronomical information which, even in the Hellenistic age, was known to be flawed.

'Those who delight in the contemplation of truth. For philosophy is not in geometry, with its postulates and hypotheses; nor in music, which is conjectural; nor in astronomy, crammed full of physical, fluid, and probable causes. But the knowledge of the good and truth itself is essential for a philosopher. He must know, on one hand, what is good, and on the other hand, the ways to the good. This is so that he does not allow the curriculum of training to be a substitute for the good.'"

Therefore, even if men say that the Greeks came upon some utterances of the true philosophy by some accident or a stroke of good fortune, nevertheless it is the accident of a divine origins and good fortune is not unforeseen. If on the other hand, one were to say that the Greeks possessed a natural conception of these things, we know that all things natural come from the Creator. That is why we call righteousness and law "natural." If some say that the Greeks had a common intellect, let us reflect who is its father, and what concepts of righteousness all minds hold in common.

CHAPTER XX.— HOW PHILOSOPHY CONTRIBUTES TO THE COMPREHENSION OF DIVINE TRUTH.

As many men drawing down the ship, cannot be called many causes, but one cause consisting of many;—for each individual by himself is not the cause of the ship being drawn, but along with the rest;—so also philosophy, being the search for truth, contributes to the comprehension of truth; not as being the cause of comprehension, but a cause along with other things, and co-operator; perhaps also a joint cause. Just as the several virtues together bring about and cause the happiness of one individual; and as both the sun, and the fire, and the bath, and clothing bring about one getting warm: so while truth is one thing, many things contribute to its investigation. But its actual discovery is by the Son. Virtue then, if we consider rightly, is only one thing known by various names. For when virtue is exhibited in one activity we might call it "prudence," and in another "self-control," and in still others "manliness" or "righteousness. . . . "

But if philosophy, through its various studies, contributes remotely to the discovery of truth, by reaching after knowledge which is related to that true knowledge that we possess,[18] then apprehending that knowledge (philosophy) in accordance with the Word, aids him who aims⌐⌐⌐⌐⌐.

---

18   By this he means faith in Christ.

The Nicene Creed

Introduction by Danya Furda (2016).

A creed is a doctrinal statement about correct beliefs, or orthodoxy. The Nicene Creed was created at the First Council of Nicaea in 325 CE to argue against Arianism and was later expanded at the Second Council of Constantinople in 381 CE. Arius was a priest from Alexandria, Egypt, who argued that Jesus was not divine in the same way as God. (The Father was the father and the Son was lesser as his son.) He thought that equating Jesus with God weakened Christianity's monotheism. Against Arius's arguments, the bishops at the Council of Nicaea professed that Jesus and God were equally divine, as was the Holy Spirit, thus affirming the doctrine of the Trinity.

Another controversy surrounding the Nicene Creed is over the filioque ("and from the Son") clause. Around 589 CE, a church council in Toledo, Spain, added this clause to the Nicene Creed, indicating that the Holy Spirit proceeded from the Son as well as from the Father, perhaps as a way to strengthen the doctrine of the Trinity. When the Roman Catholic and Orthodox split in 1054, one of the arguments for this "great schism" was over the addition of the filioque clause to the original creed. Today, Roman Catholics and Protestants say the Nicene Creed with the filioque clause while Orthodox Christians use the creed in its original form.

The Nicene Creed is the only universal and ecumenical creed in Christianity. It is the only creed used in the Orthodox Church. Roman Catholics and Protestants use the Nicene Creed in their liturgy but also recite the shorter Apostles' Creed.

We believe in one God,
the Father, the Almighty,
make of heaven and earth,
of all that is, seen and unseen.
We believe in one Lord, Jesus Christ,
the only Son of God.
eternally begotten of the Father,
God from God, Light from Light,
true God from true God,
begotten, not made,
of one Being with the Father.
Through Him all things were made.

For us and for our salvation
He became incarnate from the Virgin Mary,
And was made man.
For our sake He was crucified under Pontius Pilate;
He suffered death and was buried.
On the third day He rose again
in accordance with the scriptures;
He ascended into heaven
and is seated at the right hand of the Father.
He will come again in glory to judge the living and the dead,
and His kingdom will have no end.
We believe in the Holy Spirit, the Lord, the giver of life,
who proceeds from the Father.*
With the Father and the Son He is worshipped and glorified.
He has spoken through the prophets.
We believe in one holy catholic and apostolic church.
We acknowledge one baptism for the forgiveness of sins.
We look for the resurrection of the dead,
and the life of the world to come. Amen.

*Roman Catholics and Protestants add "and the Son" at this point.

Augustine of Hippo

Selections from *The City of God*

Translated by Marcus Dodds, in Augustine, *The City of God* (Edinburgh: T. & T. Clark, 1871).
Edited by Mark S. Bocija

St. Augustine (354-430) is the most important of the Latin Church Fathers. His ideas formed the foundation of the Christian worldview throughout the Middle Ages. He was born Tagaste in North Africa and became bishop of the city of Hippo. His literary output was enormous in an age when writing was both expensive and time consuming. Among his most important works are The Confessions, *the first autobiography in the West, and* The Enchiridion, *a handbook on Christian ethics and doctrine. He began writing* The City of God *in 410, after Alaric and the Vandals had sacked Rome. Pagan Romans blamed Christians for turning the gods against them, but Christians were nervous too.*

Why would God allow such calamities to befall his people? Both pagan and Christian political thought were predicated on the assumption that political stability and prosperity were results of being right with the gods/God, and that, conversely, disaster was a sign of apostasy. The collapse of the Roman Empire necessitated a radical rethinking of the nature of the state. In The City of God, *Augustine provides new paradigms for how Christian society will conceive of the state and the place of the individual in society.*

That the Misfortunes of Rome are Not Caused by Christians

But remember that, in recounting these things, I have still to address myself to ignorant men; so ignorant, indeed, as to give birth to the common saying: "Drought and Christianity go hand in hand." There are indeed some among them who are thoroughly well-educated men, and have a taste for history, in which the things I speak of are open to their observation; but in order to irritate the uneducated masses against us, they feign ignorance of these events, and do what they can to make the vulgar believe that those disasters, which in certain places and at certain times uniformly befall mankind, are the result of Christianity, which is being everywhere diffused, and is possessed of a renown and brilliancy which quite eclipse their own gods. Let them then, along with us, call to mind with what various and repeated disasters the prosperity of Rome was blighted, before ever Christ had come in the flesh, and before His name had been blazoned among the nations with that glory which they vainly grudge. Let them, if they can, defend their gods in this article, since they maintain that they worship them in order to be preserved from these disasters, which they now blame on us whenever they suffer them in the least degree. For why did these gods permit the disasters I am to speak of to fall on their worshippers before the preaching of Christ's name offended them?

All Power Given and Taken by God for His Own Reasons

These things being so, we do not attribute the power of giving kingdoms and empires to any power save to the true God, who gives happiness in the kingdom of heaven to the pious alone, but gives kingly power on earth both to the pious and the impious, as it may please Him. . . . He, therefore, who is the one true God, who never leaves the human race without just judgment and help, gave a kingdom to the Romans when He determined it and He made it as great as He desired it to be. He did same to the Assyrians, and even the Persians, by whom, as their own books testify, only two gods are worshipped, the one good and the other evil,--to say nothing concerning the Hebrew

151

people, of whom I have already spoken as much as seemed necessary, who, as long as they were a kingdom, worshipped none save the true God. . . . And the same is true in respect of men as well as nations. He who gave power to Marius gave it also to Caius Caesar; He who gave it to Augustus gave it also to Nero; He also who gave it to the most benignant emperors, the Vespasians, father and son, gave it also to the cruel Domitian; and, finally, to avoid the necessity of going over them all, He who gave it to the Christian Constantine gave it also to the apostate Julian, whose gifted mind was deceived by a sacrilegious and detestable curiosity, stimulated by the love of power.

On the Wickedness of Human Nature

This life of ours—if a life so full of such great ills can properly be called a life—bears witness to the fact that, from its very start, the race of mortal men has been a race condemned. Think, first, of the dreadful abyss of ignorance from which all error flows and so engulfs the sons of Adam in a darksome pool that no one can escape without the toll of toils and tears and fears.[19] Then, take our very love for all those things that prove so vain and poisonous and breed so many heartaches, troubles, griefs, and fears; such insane joys in discord, strife, and wars; such fraud and theft and robbery; such perfidy and pride, envy and ambition, homicide and murder, cruelty and savagery, lawlessness and lust; all the shameless passions of the impure—fornication and adultery, incest and unnatural sins, rape and countless other kinds of uncleanliness too nasty to be mentioned; the sins against religion—sacrilege and heresy, blasphemy and perjury; the iniquities against our neighbors—calumnies and cheating, lies and false witness, violence to persons and property; the injustices of the courts and the innumerable other miseries and maladies that fill the world, yet escape attention.

---

19 This is referring to the doctrine of Original Sin first put forth by Paul but developed in Augustine's theology. In this context, Augustine incorporated original sin into his political vision. Because humans are broken and prone to wickedness, the coercive power of the state becomes the necessary instrument on earth to restrain human behavior. But, since the leaders of the state are no better than the rest of us, it, too, is prone to wickedness.

Of the Nature of the Two Cities, the Earthly and the Heavenly[20]

Accordingly, two cities have been formed by two loves: the earthly city by the love of self, even to the contempt of God; the heavenly by the love of God, even to the contempt of self. The former (the earthly city) glories in itself, but the latter (the heavenly city) in the Lord. For the one seeks glory from men; but the greatest glory of the other is God, the witness of conscience. The one lifts up its head in its own glory; the other says to its God, "You are my glory, and the lifter up of my head." In the earthly city the princes and the nations are ruled by the love of ruling; in the heavenly city the princes and the subjects serve one another in love, the latter obeying, while the former take thought for all. The earthly city delights in its own power represented in the persons of its rulers; the heavenly city says to its God, "I will love Thee, O Lord, my strength." And therefore the wise men of the earthly city live according to man . . . and those who have known God "glorified Him not as God, they became fools, and changed the glory of the incorruptible God into an image made to look like corruptible man, and birds, and four-footed beasts, and creeping things. But in the heavenly city there is no human wisdom, but only godliness, which offers due worship to the true God, and looks for its reward in the society of the saints, of holy angels as well as holy men, "that God may be all in all."

The earthly city is necessary for the order

But the families which do not live by faith seek their peace in the earthly advantages of this life; while the families which live by faith look for those eternal blessings which are promised, and use as pilgrims such advantages of time and of earth as do not fascinate and divert them from God, but rather aid them to endure with greater ease, and to keep down the number of those burdens of the corruptible body which weigh upon the soul. Thus the things necessary for this mortal life are used by both kinds of men and families alike, but each has its own peculiar and widely different aim in using them. The earthly city does not live by faith, seeks an earthly peace, and the end

---

20   In this section, Augustine contrasts those individuals who focus their energy on establishing the greatness of the earthly city (the state) with those who concern themselves with the heavenly city. In his judgment, the first is driven by pride, the desire for greatness, and appearances of glory, the second is governed by true devotion to God. He reminds the reader that only the heavenly city is eternal.

it proposes, in the well-ordered concord of civic obedience and rule, is the combination of men's wills to attain the things which are helpful to this life. The heavenly city, or rather the part of it which sojourns on earth and lives by faith, makes use of this peace only because it must, until this mortal condition which necessitates it shall pass away. Consequently, so long as it lives like a captive and a stranger in the earthly city, though it has already received the promise of redemption, and the gift of the Spirit as the earnest of it, it does not hesitate to obey the laws of the earthly city, whereby the things necessary for the maintenance of this mortal life are administered; and thus, as this life is common to both cities, so there is a harmony between them in regard to what belongs to it.

The believer is a citizen of the heavenly city, but just a visitor to the earthly city

Even the heavenly city, therefore, while in its state of pilgrimage, avails itself of the peace of earth, and, so far as it can without injuring faith and godliness, desires and maintains a common agreement among men regarding the acquisition of the necessaries of life, and makes this earthly peace bear upon the peace of heaven; for this alone can be truly called and esteemed the peace of the reasonable creatures, consisting as it does in the perfectly ordered and harmonious enjoyment of God and of one another in God. When we shall have reached that peace, this mortal life shall give place to one that is eternal, and our body shall be no more this animal body which by its corruption weighs down the soul, but a spiritual body feeling no want, and in all its members subjected to the will. In its pilgrim state the heavenly city possesses this peace by faith; and by this faith it lives righteously when it refers to the attainment of that peace every good action towards God and man; for the life of the city is a social life.

Pseudo-Dionysius

From *The Works of Dionysius the Areopagite*, translated by John Parker (1897).
Introduction by Tim Davis (2010).

The Celestial Hierarchy

The Celestial Hierarchy *is part of a late-fifth or early-sixth century body of*
literature which would later become known as the Corpus Areopagiticum.
These texts were composed in Greek, likely in the area around Syria and
reflect elements of **Neo-Platonic** *philosophy, the evolving controversial issues*
of Christian theology, along with components of mysticism. The first section
of The Celestial Hierarchy *creates a descriptive framework for a Christian*
understanding of angels. It also deals with symbols in the Judeo-Christian
scriptures that have shaped the medieval theory of angels while cautioning
against an over-literal interpretation of these symbols. In describing the beings
of the heavens, Dionysius includes three classes, three functions, and three levels.
In addition to proposing a framework for understanding the angelic beings, The
Celestial Hierarchy *sets the tone for the development of angelology in the West.*
The work's influence in the areas of art and architecture from the Middle Ages
through the Renaissance is quite significant. The three-fold grouping of angels
presented by Dionysius is repeated in medieval theology from the late-sixth
century through the 1400's.

Chapter One, Part 2 - *The Celestial Hierarchy*

We must lift up the immaterial and steady eyes of our minds to that outpouring
of Light which is so primal, indeed much more so, and which comes from
source of divinity, I mean the Father. This is the Light which, by way of
representative symbols, makes known to us the most blessed hierarchies
among the angels . . .

Chapter Four, Part 4 - *The Celestial Hierarchy*

Jesus himself, the transcendent Cause of those beings which
live beyond the world, came to take on human form without in any
way changing his own essential nature. But I observe that never once
did he abandon that human form which he had established and chosen,
and he obediently submitted to the wishes of God the Father as
arranged by the angels.

Chapter Six, Part 2 - *The Celestial Hierarchy*

. . . the first group is forever around God and is said to be permanently united with him ahead
of any of the others and with no intermediary. Here, then, are the
most holy "thrones" and the orders said to possess many eyes and
many wings, called in Hebrew the "cherubim" and "seraphim." Following
the tradition of Scripture, he says that they are found immediately
around God and in a proximity enjoyed by no other . . .

Chapter Six, Part 2 - *The Celestial Hierarchy*

The second group, he says, is made up of "authorities," "dominions,"
and "powers." And the third, at the end of the heavenly hierarchies,
is the group of "angels," "archangels," and "principalities."

Chapter Nine, Part 2 - *The Celestial Hierarchy*

As I have already said, the angels complete the entire ranking of
the heavenly intelligences. Among the heavenly beings it is they who
possess the final quality of being an angel. For being closer to us, they,
more appropriately than the previous ones, are named "angels" insofar
as their hierarchy is more concerned with revelation and is closer to the world.

John of Damascus, *On Holy Images* (c. 730)

From St. John Damascene *On Holy Images*, translated by Mary H. Allies (London: Thomas Baker, 1898), pp. 10-17. Revised and introduced by Mark S. Bocija

The prohibition against graven images in the Ten Commandments was a core feature of Jewish religious identity and was preserved in Islamic culture as well. Christians tended to interpret the prohibition more loosely, and as early as the second century images or icons of Christ and the saints began to appear. By the fourth century, a formal typology of traits had already emerged. These images had their origins in Hellenistic funeral portraits and were originally commemorative in nature. But in the East they became objects of veneration and were incorporated into liturgy. Individuals called "iconoclasts" (image breakers) demanded the destruction of icons and gained an ally with the ascension of Emperor Leo III (717-741) who in 726 initiated a prohibition on the use of religious images. The resulting Iconoclastic Controversy bitterly divided the Eastern Church until 843 when Empress Theodora allowed their restoration. During this time, a number of defenses of icons were made based on Platonic metaphysics. The following selection is from St. John of Damascus (c.675-c.749), one of the most important defenders of icons. John lived during Leo's suppression of icons but was able to write freely since he lived under Muslim rule outside the boundaries of the Byzantine emperor. John's commentary goes beyond the defense of icons and provides us with an eloquent and profound investigation into the nature of art.

Now, as we are talking of images and worship, let us analyze the exact meaning of each. An image is a likeness or picture of the original with a certain difference, for it is not an *exact* reproduction of the original. In the same way, the Son (Christ) is the living, substantial, Image of the invisible God, bearing in Himself the whole Father, being in all things equal to Him, differing only in being begotten by the Father, who is the Begetter; the Son is begotten [21]. . . . Again, visible things are images of invisible and intangible things, on which they throw a faint light. Holy Scripture clothes in figure God and the angels, and the Blessed Denis[22] explains why. When sensible things

---

21 It is important to understand this terminology. According to Christian theology, Christ was "begotten, not made." Therefore he shares the same essence or being as the Father. 400 years earlier, the Nicean Creed stated the Christ was "begotten not made, one in being with the Father."

22 He is referring to a neo-Platonic writer of the late fifth century Pseudo-Dionysius the Areopagite. His real name and just about everything else about him is unknown. In John's time he was popularly misidentified as the martyr of Gaul, St. Denis, the first Bishop of Paris.

clearly illustrate what is beyond our senses, they give a material form to what is intangible. We would consider any medium[23] to be imperfect if it did not sufficiently represent a material vision, or if it required effort to recognize it. Likewise, Holy Scripture presents us with many things that are intangible, but clothes them in flesh. By clothing spiritual things in flesh[24], does it not make an image of something invisible by using what is familiar to our nature and in doing so bring invisible things down to the level of our understanding? A certain conception through the senses thus takes place in the brain, which was not there before, and is transmitted to the judicial faculty, and added to the mental store.

Gregory, who is so eloquent about God, says that the mind always strives to go beyond corporeal things, but is incapable of doing it. Since the beginning, God has made himself visible to us through physical images. We see images in creation which remind us faintly of God. Just as when we associate the holiness of God with the sun, or light, or burning rays, or with a running fountain, or a full river, or with the mind, or with speech, or with the spirit within us, or with a rose tree, or a sprouting flower, or a sweet fragrance.

Of old[25], God the incorporeal was never depicted. But now, however, when God has been seen clothed in flesh, and conversing with men, if I make an image of the God whom I see (Christ) that does not mean that I worship matter. Rather, I worship the God of matter, who became matter for my sake, and deigned to inhabit matter, who worked out my salvation through matter. I will not cease from honoring that matter which works my salvation. I venerate it, though not as God. How could God be born out of lifeless things? And if God's body is God by union, it is immutable. The nature of God remains the same as before, the flesh created in time is quickened by, a logical and reasoning soul.

---

23 In art, *medium* refers to the particular materials (clay, paint, stone etc.) along with its accompanying techniques that are employed by the artist.

24 By flesh he means more generally any "physical form," but the use of the word "flesh" is meant to be evocative of the incarnation of Christ as God made Flesh, which ultimately is his justification for crafting of images.

25 In this paragraph he gets to the meat of his argument. "Of old" refers to the Old Testament period which he contrasts with "Now," the time after Christ. The incarnation of Christ has made the old prohibition of images irrelevant.

I honor all matter besides, and venerate it. . . . Was not the blessed wood of the Cross matter? Was not the sacred and holy mountain of Calvary matter? What of the life-giving rock, the Holy Sepulchre[26], the source of our resurrection: was it not matter? Is not the most holy book of the Gospels matter? Is not the blessed table matter which gives us the Bread of Life? Are not the gold and silver matter, out of which crosses and altar-plate and chalices are made? And before all these things, is not the body and blood of our Lord matter? Either do away with the veneration and worship due to all these things, or submit to the tradition of the Church in the worship of images, honoring God and His friends, and following in this the grace of the Holy Spirit.

The Conversion of Europe

Christianity in the Roman period had been an urban movement, but in the countryside, especially in German lands where Roman civilization scarcely penetrated, Christianity was largely unknown. In other territories such as England, the veneer of Roman-Christian civilization had been wiped away by the migration of the Germanic Anglos and Saxons. In the Early Middle Ages, these marginal territories became Christianized largely due to the efforts of monks. Pope Gregory I the Great sent monks to England to preach the faith. Later Anglo-Saxon monks like Boniface braved many dangers and eventually converted much of northern Europe to Christianity. The readings below illustrate the complex nature of religious conversion at this time. Evidently, their efforts met with some initial success. Christianity had a certain appeal because Christ had been the God of the Roman emperors, but naturally even those who accepted the new faith did not change everything about themselves overnight. Some returned to the old faith, others accepted Christianity but simply grafted it on to their existing religious practices. In other words, they were willing to add "the Great God Jesus" into their pantheon, but did not change their fundamental religious outlook. The passages below represent two very different responses these challenges. Note that Gregory and Boniface have very different approaches to the difficulties of converting of pagan peoples.

---

26 The tomb in which Christ's body was placed. Constantine had a monumental church built over the tomb. The stone bench on which, according to tradition, Christ body was laid out is preserved in situ in the church and has since been an object of veneration. This is the "rock" he is referring to.

Gregory the Great on the Conversion of the Pagans

From the Venerable Bede, *History of the English Church and People* in J. H. Robinson, *Readings in European History*, (Boston: Ginn, 1905), pp. 97-105. Introduction by Mark Bocija.

At the beginning of the seventh century, Pope Gregory I sent a small group of Benedictine monks to England to preach the Gospels to the Anglo-Saxons. His advice to the missionaries he sent to England demonstrates a sensitivity to and insight into human nature that allowed for assimilation and a redefinition of cultural practices in line with Christian doctrine.

To our well loved son Abbot Mellitus: Gregory, servant of the servants of God.

"Since the departure of those of our fellowship who are bearing you company, we have been seriously anxious, because we have received no news of your journey. Therefore, when by God's help you reach our most reverend brother, Bishop Augustine, we wish you to inform him that we have been giving careful thought to the affairs of the English, and have come to the conclusion that the temples of the idols among that people should on no account be destroyed. The idols are to be destroyed, but the temples themselves are to be aspersed with holy water, altars set up in them, and relics deposited there. For if these temples are well-built, they must be purified from the worship of demons and dedicated to the service of the true God. In this way, we hope that the people, seeing that their temples are not destroyed, may abandon their error and, flocking more readily to their accustomed resorts, may come to know and adore the true God. And since they have a custom of sacrificing many oxen to demons, let some other solemnity be substituted in its place, such as a day of Dedication or the Festivals of the holy martyrs whose relics are enshrined there. On such occasions they might well construct shelters of boughs for themselves around the churches that were once temples, and celebrate the solemnity with devout feasting. They are no longer to sacrifice beasts to the Devil, but they may kill them for food to the praise of God, and give thanks to the Giver of all gifts for the plenty they enjoy. If the people are allowed some worldly pleasures in this way, they will more readily come to desire the joys of the spirit. For it is certainly impossible to eradicate all errors from obstinate minds at one stroke, and whoever wished to climb to a mountain top climbs gradually step by step, and not in one leap. It was in this way that the Lord revealed Himself to the Israelite people in Egypt, permitting the sacrifices formerly offered to the Devil to be offered thenceforward to Himself instead. . . .

160

From the *Life of St. Boniface* by Willibald

C. H. Talbot, *The Anglo-Saxon Missionaries in Germany, Being the Lives of SS. Willibrord, Boniface, Leoba and Lebuin together with the Hodoepericon of St. Willibald and a selection from the correspondence of St. Boniface*, (London and New York: Sheed and Ward, 1954). Introduction by Mark Bocija.

Willibald's Life of Boniface records the activities of one of the most significant movements of the Early Middle Ages. Anglo-Saxon monks, like their Irish counterparts, saw themselves as pilgrims in the this world and frequently took on the life of a wandering evangelist, going into pagan lands, preaching the Gospels, and establishing Christian communities. This was dangerous work in an untamed land. Many monks were promptly robbed and killed. Some, like Boniface, had long, successful careers, and then were robbed and killed. The following is one of the most dramatic scenes from Willibald's biography of Boniface. In almost all pagan traditions, religion was a practical matter. Gods were powerful beings whose worshippers believed would, if properly propitiated, help them defeat their enemies and make them prosper. Boniface's actions in the following excerpt are meant to challenge the power of the pagan deities.

Now many of the Hessians who at that time had acknowledged the Catholic faith were confirmed by the grace of the Holy Spirit and received the laying-on of hands. But others, not yet strong in the spirit, refused to accept the pure teachings of the church in their entirety. Moreover, some continued secretly, others openly, to offer sacrifices to trees and springs, to inspect the entrails of victims; some practiced divination, *legerdemain*[27], and incantations; some turned their attention to auguries[28], auspices, and other sacrificial rites; while others, of a more reasonable character, forsook all the profane practices of the Gentiles [i.e., pagans] and committed none of these crimes. With the counsel and advice of the latter persons, Boniface in their presence attempted to cut down, at a place called Gaesmere, a certain oak of extraordinary size called in the old tongue of the pagans the Oak of Jupiter.[29] Taking his courage in his hands (for a great crowd of pagans stood by watching and bitterly cursing in their hearts the enemy of the gods), he cut the first notch. But when he had

---

27   *Ligerdemain* means magic, but magic that is deceptive or sleight-of –hand. The force of the word here is meant to indicate that those who practice it are engaged in trickery to mislead others.

28   The practice of reading signs or omens in order to predict the future.

29   This is an error on the part of Willibald. The tree was the home of Thor or Odin. Willibald was unfamiliar with Germanic religion and therefore assumes that these German pagans worship the Greco-Roman deities.

made a superficial cut. Suddenly, the oak's vast bulk, shaken by a mighty blast of wind from above crashed to the ground shivering its topmost branches into fragments in its fall. As if by the express will of God (for the brethren present had done nothing to cause it) the oak burst asunder into four parts, each part having a trunk of equal length. At the sight of this extraordinary spectacle the heathens who had been cursing ceased to revile and began, on the contrary, to believe and bless the Lord.

St. Francis of Assisi

"THE CANTICLE OF THE SUN"

From *The Writings of St. Francis of Assisi*, translated by Paschal Robinson, (1905), at sacred-texts.com. Introduction by Tim Davis (2016).

"The Canticle of the Sun" was composed as a hymn of praise by St. Francis of Assisi around 1224 (the year he supposedly received the stigmata of Christ). It was written in Italian, likely in an Umbrian dialect, and has been preserved in the early Franciscan tradition. Many versions have been adapted, paraphrased, and re-echoed throughout all corners of Christianity, into our modern devotion today. Tradition says he composed the hymn at a tiny cottage in San Damiano where he was attempting to recover from a serious illness. According to first generation Franciscan biographer Thomas of Celano, the hymn was sung by two of his oldest companions at Francis's deathbed. St. Francis's belief that nature was the mirror of God and that all things are connected through the Creator continued to be embraced throughout the Christian tradition and continue to popularly persist in a number of contemporary ecological movements that are ideologically rooted in faith.

HERE BEGIN THE PRAISES OF THE CREATURES WHICH THE BLESSED FRANCIS MADE TO THE PRAISE AND HONOR OF GOD WHILE HE WAS ILL AT ST. DAMIAN'S:

Most high, omnipotent, good Lord,
Praise, glory and honor and benediction all, are Yours.
To Thee alone do they belong, most High,
And there is no man fit to mention Thee.
Praise be to Thee, my Lord, with all Thy creatures,
Especially to my worshipful brother sun,

The which lights up the day, and through him does Thou brightness give;
And beautiful is he and radiant with splendor great;
Of Thee, most High, signification gives.
Praised be my Lord, for sister moon and for the stars,
In heaven Thou hast formed them clear and precious and fair.
Praised be my Lord for brother wind
And for the air and clouds and fair and every kind of weather,
By the which Thou gives to Thy creatures nourishment.
Praised be my Lord for sister water,
The which is greatly helpful and humble and precious and pure.
Praised be my Lord for brother fire,
By the which Thou lightest up the dark.
And fair is he and gay and mighty and strong.
Praised be my Lord for our sister, mother earth,
The which sustains and keeps us
And brings forth diverse fruits with grass and flowers bright.
Praised be my Lord for those who for Thy love forgive
And weakness bear and tribulation.
Blessed those who shall in peace endure,
For by Thee, most High, shall they be crowned.
Praised be my Lord for our sister, the bodily death,
From the which no living man can flee.
Woe to them who die in mortal sin;
Blessed those who shall find themselves in Thy most holy will,
For the second death shall do them no ill.
Praise ye and bless ye my Lord, and give Him thanks,
And be subject unto Him with great humility.

pp. 152-153

St. Francis and the Mirror of Perfection

From Brother Leo's Stories of St. Francis

Chapter 4 - On the Novice Who Sought Permission to Own a Psalter

At another time a friar novice who knew how to recite the psalter (a book of biblical psalms, especially for liturgical use), although not fluently, obtained leave from the Minister General to have his own copy. But having heard that blessed Francis did not wish his friars to hanker after learning and books, he was not happy about having it without his permission. So when blessed Francis was visiting the friary to which this novice belonged, the novice said to him, 'Father, it would give me great pleasure to have a psalter. But although the Minister General has granted permission, I would like to have it with your approval.' To which blessed Francis replied, 'The Emperor Charles, Roland, Oliver, and all the paladins and men of valor were mighty in battle, fought the Infidels until death with great sweat and toil, and they gained a famous victory. And the holy martyrs themselves gave their lives in battle for the Faith of Christ. But in these days there are many who wish to win honor and praise from men by merely telling of their deeds. In the same way, there are many among us who want to win honor and praise by merely proclaiming and reciting the deeds of the Saints.' As though to say, 'Our concern is not with books and learning, but with holy deeds; for learning brings pride, but charity edifies.'

Some days later, as blessed Francis was sitting by the fire, the novice spoke to him again about the psalter. And blessed Francis said to him, 'Once you have a psalter, you will want a breviary. And when you have a breviary, you will sit in a high chair like a great prelate, and say to your brother, "Bring me my breviary!"' As he spoke, blessed Francis in great fervor of spirit took up a handful of ashes and placed them on his head, and rubbing his hand around his head as though he was washing it, he exclaimed, 'I a breviary! I, a breviary!, I a breviary!' And he repeated this many times, passing his hand over his head. And the friar was amazed and ashamed.

The 95 Theses

Published in: *Works of Martin Luther*, Adolph Spaeth, L.D. Reed, Henry Eyster Jacobs, et Al., Trans. & Eds. (Philadelphia: A. J. Holman Company, 1915), Vol. 1, pp. 29-38.

DISPUTATION OF DOCTOR MARTIN LUTHER
ON THE POWER AND EFFICACY OF INDULGENCES

OCTOBER 31, 1517

Out of love for the truth and the desire to bring it to light, the following propositions will be discussed at Wittenberg, under the presidency of the Reverend Father Martin Luther,

Master of Arts and of Sacred Theology, and Lecturer in Ordinary on the same at that place. Wherefore he requests that those who are unable to be present and debate orally with us, may do so by letter.

In the Name our Lord Jesus Christ. Amen.

1. Our Lord and Master Jesus Christ, when He said *Poenitentiam agite* (repent and do penance), willed that the whole life of believers should be repentance.

2. This word cannot be understood to mean sacramental penance, i.e., confession and satisfaction, which is administered by the priests.

3. Yet it means not inward repentance only; nay, there is no inward repentance which does not outwardly work diverse mortifications of the flesh.

4. The penalty [of sin], therefore, continues so long as hatred of self continues; for this is the true inward repentance, and continues until our entrance into the kingdom of heaven.

....

8. The penitential canons are imposed only on the living, and, according to them, nothing should be imposed on the dying.

9. Therefore the Holy Spirit in the pope is kind to us, because in his decrees he always makes exception of the article of death and of necessity.

10. Ignorant and wicked are the doings of those priests who, in the case of the dying, reserve canonical penances for purgatory.

11. This changing of the canonical penalty to the penalty of purgatory is quite evidently one of the tares that were sown while the bishops slept.

. . . .

21. Therefore those preachers of indulgences are in error, who say that by the pope's indulgences a man is freed from every penalty, and saved;

22. Whereas he remits to souls in purgatory no penalty which, according to the canons, they would have had to pay in this life.

. . . .

24. It must need be, therefore, that the greater part of the people are deceived by that indiscriminate and high sounding promise of release from penalty.

. . . .

27. They preach man who say that so soon as the penny jingles into the money-box, the soul flies out [of purgatory].

28. It is certain that when the penny jingles into the money-box, gain and avarice can be increased, but the result of the intercession of the Church is in the power of God alone.

. . . .

30. No one is sure that his own contrition is sincere; much less that he has attained full remission.

31. Rare as is the man that is truly penitent, so rare is also the man who truly buys indulgences, i.e., such men are most rare.

32. They will be condemned eternally, together with their teachers, who believe themselves sure of their salvation because they have letters of pardon.

. . . .

35. They preach no Christian doctrine who teach that contrition is not necessary in those who intend to buy souls out of purgatory or to buy the things of confession.

36. Every truly repentant Christian has a right to full remission of penalty and guilt, even without letters of pardon.

37. Every true Christian, whether living or dead, has part in all the blessings of Christ and the Church; and this is granted him by God, even without letters of pardon.

. . . .

42. Christians are to be taught that the pope does not intend the buying of pardons to be compared in any way to works of mercy.

43. Christians are to be taught that he who gives to the poor or lends to the needy does a better work than buying pardons;

. . . .

46. Christians are to be taught that unless they have more than they need, they are bound to keep back what is necessary for their own families, and by no means to squander it on pardons.

. . . .

52. The assurance of salvation by letters of pardon is vain, even though the commissary, nay, even though the pope himself, were to stake his soul upon it.

. . . .

56. The "treasures of the Church," out of which the pope grants indulgences, are not sufficiently named or known among the people of Christ.

. . . .

62. The true treasure of the Church is the Most Holy Gospel of the glory and the grace of God.

. . . .

68. Yet they are in truth the very smallest graces compared with the grace of God and the piety of the Cross.

. . . .

72. But he who guards against the lust and license of the pardon-preachers, let him be blessed!

....

76. We say, on the contrary, that the papal pardons are not able to remove the very least of venial sins, so far as its guilt is concerned.

....

82. To wit:--"Why does not the pope empty purgatory, for the sake of holy love and of the dire need of the souls that are there, if he redeems an infinite number of souls for the sake of miserable money with which to build a Church? The former reasons would be most just; the latter is most trivial."

....

86. Again:--"Why does not the pope, whose wealth is today greater than the riches of the richest, build just this one church of St. Peter with his own money, rather than with the money of poor believers?"

....

92. Away, then, with all those prophets who say to the people of Christ, "Peace, peace," and there is no peace!

13

Islam

THE QUR'ÂN

Translated by E.H. Palmer in *Sacred Books of the East*, Vol. 6 (1880) at sacred-texts.com. Introduction and editing by Tim Davis (2016).

THE OPENING CHAPTER.
I Mecca

In the name of the merciful and compassionate God.

Praise belongs to God, the Lord of the worlds, the merciful, the compassionate, the ruler of the day of judgment! Thee we serve and Thee we ask for aid. [5] Guide us in the right path, the path of those Thou art gracious to; not of those Thou art angry with; nor of those who err.

THE CHAPTER OF THE BEE
XVI Mecca

In the name of the merciful and compassionate God.

God's bidding will come; seek not then to hasten it on. Celebrated be His praises from what they join with Him!

He sends down the angels with the Spirit at His bidding upon whom He will of His servants (to say), 'Give warning that there is no god but Me; Me therefore do ye fear.' He created the heavens and the earth in truth! Exalted be He above that which they join with Him.

He created man from a clot; and yet, behold, he is an open opponent!

[5] The cattle too have we created for you; in them is warmth and profit, and from them do you eat.

In them is there beauty for you when ye drive them home to rest, and when ye drive them forth to graze. And they bear your heavy burdens to towns which ye could not otherwise reach, except with great wretchedness of soul; verily, your Lord is kind and merciful.

And horses too, and mules, and asses, for you to ride upon and for an ornament.. He creates also what you know not of. God's it is to show the path; from it some turn aside: but had He pleased, He would have guided you one and all.

[10] He it is who sends down water from the sky, whence you have drink, and whence the trees grow whereby you feed your flocks.

He makes the corn to grow, and the olives, and the palms, and the grapes, and some of every fruit; verily, in that is a sign unto a people who reflect.

And He subjected to you the night and the day, and the sun, and the moon, and the stars are subjected to His bidding. Verily, in that are signs to a people who have sense.

And what He has produced for you in the earth varying in hue, verily, in that is a sign for a people who are mindful.

THE CHAPTER OF THE PILGRIMAGE.
(XXII Mecca)

Translated by E.H. Palmer in *Sacred Books of the East*, Vol. 9 (1880) at sacred-texts.com.

[25] Verily, those who misbelieve and who turn men away from God's path and the Sacred Mosque, which we have made for all men alike, the dweller therein, and the stranger, and he who desires therein profanation with injustice, we will make him taste grievous woe.

And when we established for Abraham the place of the House, (saying), 'Associate naught with me, but cleanse my House for those who make the circuits, for those who stand to pray, for those who bow, and for those too who adore.

'And proclaim amongst men the Pilgrimage; let them come to you on foot and on every slim camel, from every deep pass, that they may witness advantages for them, and may mention the name of God for the stated days over what God has provided them with brute beasts, then eat thereof, and feed those badly off, the poor.

[30] 'Then let them finish the neglect of their person, and let them pay their vows and make the circuit round the old House.

'That do. And who so magnifies the sacred things of God, it is better for him with his Lord.

…………………………

[50] Those who strive to discredit our signs, they are the fellows of hell!'

We have not sent before thee any apostle or prophet, but that when he wished, Satan threw not something into his wish; but it is God who annuls what Satan throws; then does God confirm his signs. God is knowing, wise to make what Satan throws as a trial unto those in whose hearts is sickness; and those whose hearts are hard; and, verily, the wrong-doers are in a wide schism. Those who have been given 'the knowledge' may know that it is the truth from thy Lord, and may believe therein, and that their hearts may be lowly; for, verily, God surely will guide those who believe into a right way.

But those who misbelieve will not cease to be in doubt thereof until the Hour comes on them suddenly, or there comes on them the torment of the barren day.

[55] The kingdom on that day shall be God's, He shall judge between them; and those who believe and do aright shall be in gardens of pleasure, but those who misbelieve and say our signs are lies, for them is shameful woe.

pp. 61-63

THE CHAPTER OF PROHIBITION
LXVI Medînah

O you who believe, turn contrite to God with sincere repentance; it may be that thy Lord will cover for you your offences and will bring you into gardens beneath which rivers flow! The day God will not disgrace the Prophet nor those who believe with him; their light shall run on before them, and at their right hands they shall say, 'Our Lord, perfect for us our light and forgive us verily, Thou art mighty over all!'

O thou prophet, fight strenuously against the misbelievers and hypocrites and be stern towards them; for their resort is hell, and an evil journey shall it be!

[10] God strikes out a parable to those who misbelieve: the wife of Noah and the wife of Lot; they were under two of our righteous servants, but they betrayed them: and they availed them nothing against God; and it was said, 'Enter the fire with those who enter.'

And God strikes out a parable for those who believe: the wife of Pharaoh, when she said, 'My Lord, build for me a house with Thee in Paradise, and save me from Pharaoh and his works, and save me from the unjust people!'

And Mary (mother of Jesus), daughter of Imrân (Joachim), who guarded her private parts, and we breathed therein of our spirit and she verified the words of her Lord and His books, and was of the devout.

pp. 291-2

SURA XIX, MARY LVIII
MECCA

From the Rodwell edition of the *Quran*, (1876); at sacred-texts.com

Make mention also in the Book of Abraham; for he was a man of truth, a Prophet (Nabi).

When he said to his Father, "O my Father! why dost thou worship that which neither seeth nor heareth, nor profiteth thee?

O my Father! verily now hath knowledge come to me which hath not come to thee. Follow me therefore--I will guide thee into an even path.

O my Father! worship not Satan, for Satan is a rebel against the God of Mercy.

O my Father! indeed I fear lest a chastisement from the God of Mercy light upon thee, and thou become Satan's vassal."

He said, "Cast thou off my Gods, O Abraham? If thou forbear not, I will surely stone thee. Begone from me for a length of time."

He said, "Peace be on thee! I will pray my Lord for thy forgiveness, for he is gracious to me:

But I will separate myself from you, and the gods you call on beside God, and on my Lord will I call. My prayers to my Lord will not be with ill success."

And when he had separated himself from them and that which they worshipped beside God, we bestowed on him Isaac and Jacob, and each of them we made a prophet:

And we bestowed gifts on them in our mercy, and gave them the lofty tongue of truth."

And commemorate Moses in "the Book;" for he was a man of purity: moreover he was an Apostle, a Prophet:

From the right side of the mountain we called to him, and caused him to draw to us for secret conversation:

And we bestowed on him in our mercy his brother Aaron, a Prophet.

And commemorate Ismael in "the Book;" for he was true to his promise, and was an Apostle, a Prophet;

And he enjoined prayer and almsgiving on his people, and was well pleasing to his Lord.

And commemorate Edris (Enoch) in "the Book;" for he was a man of truth, a Prophet:

And we uplifted him to a place on high.

These are they among the prophets of the posterity of Adam, and among those whom we include with Noah, and among the posterity of Abraham and Israel, and among those whom we have guided and chosen, to whom God hath shewed favor. When the signs of the God of Mercy were rehearsed to them, they bowed them down worshipping and weeping.

On the Nature of God

From *The Koran*, translated from the Arabic by J.M. Rodwell, (London, B. Quaritch, 1876).

God, there is no god but He, the living, the self-subsistent. Slumber takes Him not, nor sleep. His is what is in the heavens and what is in the earth. Who is it that intercedes with Him save by His permission? He knows what is before them and what behind them, and they comprehend not aught of His knowledge but of what He pleases. His throne extends over the heavens and the earth, and it tires Him not to guard them both, for He is high and grand. (2:255-257)

In the name of the merciful and compassionate God. The merciful taught the Qur'an; He created man, taught him plain speech. The sun and the moon have their appointed time; the herbs and the trees adore (him). And the heavens, He raised them and set the balance, that you should not transgress the balance. But measure your actions aright, and shift not the balance. And the earth He has created for living creatures; therein are fruits and palms, with sheaths; and grain with chaff and scented herbs. Then which of your Lord's blessings would you deny? He created men from potter's clay. And He created the ginn (the spirits) from smokeless fire. Which of your Lord's blessings would you deny? (55: 1-18)

....

All that is in the heavens and the earth glorifies Allah; and He is the Mighty, the Wise.

His is the sovereignty of the heavens and the earth; He awards and He gives death; and He is able to do all things.

He is the First and the Last, and the Outward and the Inward; and He is Knower of all things.

He it is who created the heavens and the earth in six days; then He mounted the throne. He knows all that enters the earth and all that emerges from it and all that comes down from the sky and all that ascends to it; and He is with you wherever you may be. And Allah is Seer of what you do.

His is the sovereignty of the heavens and the earth, and unto Allah (all) things are brought back.

He causes the night to pass into the day, and He causes the day to pass into the night, and He is knower of all that is in the hearts of men. (57:1-7)

Righteous Conduct

From *The Koran*, translated from the Arabic by J.M. Rodwell. (London: B. Quaritch, 1876).

It is not righteousness that you turn your faces to the East or to the West; but righteous is he who believes in Allah and the Last Day and the angels and the scripture and the prophets; and gives of his wealth, for love of Him, to kinsfolk and to orphans and the needy and the wayfarer and to those who ask, and to set slaves free; and observes proper worship and pays the poor-due. And those are righteous who keep their treaty when they make one, and who are patient in tribulation and adversity and time of stress. Such are they who are true believers. Such are the God-fearing. (2:176-178)

………………………

Serve Allah and ascribe no thing as a partner unto Him. (Show) kindness to parents, and to near kindred, and orphans, and the needy, and to the neighbor who is of kin to you and to the neighbor who is not, and the fellow-traveler and the wayfarer and to the slaves whom you possess. Lo! Allah loves not those who are proud and boastful, who hoard their wealth and enjoin others to be selfish and to hide that which Allah hath bestowed upon them from His bounty. For disbelievers we prepare a shameful doom; and (also) those who spend their wealth in order to be seen of men, and do not believe in Allah nor the Last Day. He who takes Satan for a comrade, has an evil comrade.

What have they have to fear if they believe in Allah and the Last Day and spend (aright) of that which Allah has bestowed upon them, when Allah is ever aware of them (and all they do)?

Men are in charge of women, because Allah has made the one of them superior to the other, and because they spend of their property for the support of women. So women are the obedient women, guarding in secret that which Allah hath guarded. As for those from whom you fear disobedience, admonish them and banish them to their beds, and beat them. Then if they obey you, take no other action against them. Surely Allah is ever High, Exalted, Great.

And if you fear a breach between the man and wife, appoint an arbiter from his folk and an arbiter from her folk. If they desire reconciliation Allah will make them of one mind. Lo! Allah is ever Knower, Aware.

Surah 4, *An-Nisa*

On Judaism and Christianity

From *The Koran*, translated from the Arabic by J.M. Rodwell. (London: B. Quaritch, 1876).

Verily, we have sent down the law (Torah) wherein are guidance and light. By it did the prophets who professed Islam judge the Jews; and the doctors and the teachers judged by that portion of the Book of God, of which they were the keepers and the witnesses. Therefore, O Jews! Fear not men but fear Me; and barter not away my signs for a mean price! And whoso will not judge by what God hath sent down--such are the Infidels.

And in the footsteps of the prophets we brought forth Jesus, the son of Mary, to follow, confirming the law which was before him: and we gave him the Gospel with its guidance and light, confirming the Torah; a guidance and warning to those who fear God--

And to thee we have sent down the Book of the Koran with truth, confirmatory of previous Scriptures, and their safeguard. Judge therefore between them by what God hath sent down, and follow not their desires by deserting the truth which hath come unto thee. To every one of you have we given a rule and a beaten track.

And when the angels said: O Mary! Lo! Allah has chosen you and made you pure, and hath preferred you above (all) the women of creation.

O Mary! Be obedient to your Lord, prostrate yourself and bow with those who bow (in worship).

This is of the tidings of things hidden. We reveal it unto you (Muhammad). You were not present with them when they threw their pens (to know) which of them should be the guardian of Mary, nor were you present with them when they quarreled (thereupon).

(And remember) when the angels said: O Mary! Lo! Allah giveth you glad tidings of a word from him, whose name is the Messiah, Jesus, son of Mary, illustrious in the world and in the Hereafter, and one of those brought near (unto Allah).

He will speak unto mankind in his cradle and in his manhood, and he will be among the righteous.

She said: My Lord! How can I have a child when no mortal has touched me? He said: So (it will be). Allah creates what He will. If He decrees a thing, He says only: Be! and it is.

176

And He will teach him the Scripture and wisdom, and the Torah and the Gospel,

And Allah will make him (Jesus) a messenger unto the Children of Israel, (saying):

Lo! I come unto you with a sign from your Lord. Lo! I fashion for you out of clay the likeness of a bird, and I breathe into it and it is a bird, by Allah's leave. I heal him who was born blind, and the leper, and I raise the dead, by Allah's leave. And I announce unto you what you eat and what you store up in your houses. Lo! herein verily is a portent for you, if you are to be believers.

And (I come) confirming that which was before me of the Torah, and to make lawful some of that which was forbidden unto you. I come unto you with a sign from your Lord, so keep your duty to Allah and obey me.

Lo! Allah is my Lord and your Lord, so worship Him. That is a straight path.

....

Lo! The likeness of Jesus with Allah is as the likeness of Adam. He created him of dust, then He said unto him: Be! and he is.

O People of the Scripture! Why do you confound truth with falsehood and knowingly conceal the truth?

O People of the Scripture! Do not exaggerate in your religion nor utter anything concerning Allah save the truth. The Messiah, Jesus son of Mary, was only an apostle of Allah, and His word which He conveyed unto Mary, and a spirit from Him. So believe in Allah and His messengers, and say not "Three" -- Stop! (it is) better for you!--Allah is only One God. Far is it removed from His Transcendent Majesty that He should have a son. His is all that is in the heavens and all that is in the earth. And Allah is sufficient as Defender.

The Messiah (Jesus) will never disdain to be a slave unto Allah, nor do the angels who are closest to him. Those who disdain His service and are proud, all such will He assemble unto Him;

Then, as for those who believed and did good works, unto them will He pay their wages in full, adding to them out of His bounty; and as for those who were scornful and proud, them will He punish with a painful doom.

Surah 3, *Al-Imran*

The Judgment

From *The Koran*, translated from the Arabic by J.M. Rodwell. (London: B. Quaritch, 1876).

In the name of God, the Compassionate, the Merciful. When the day that must come shall have come suddenly, none shall treat that sudden coming as a lie: Day that shall abase some! Day that shall exalt others! When the earth shall be shaken with a shock, And the mountains shall be crumbled with a crumbling, and shall become scattered dust, and into three bands shall you be divided: Then the people of the right hand--Oh! how happy shall be the people of the right hand! And the people of the left hand--Oh! how wretched shall be the people of the left hand! And they who were foremost on earth--the foremost still. These are they who shall be brought close to God, in gardens of delight; a crowd from former generations and few of the latter generations; On gold-wrought couches reclining on them face to face: immortal youths will go around to them with goblets and ewers and a cup of flowing wine; their heads will not ache from it, nor their senses dim.

And with such fruits as shall please them best, and with flesh of such birds, as they shall long for: and Beautiful virgins, with large dark eyes, like pearls hidden in their shells, shall be theirs in recompense of their past labors.

They shall hear no vain discourse there, nor charge of sin, But only the greeting, "Peace! Peace!" And the people of the right hand--oh! how happy shall be the people of the right hand! Amid thornless plums and banana trees covered with fruit, and in extended shade, and by flowing waters, and with abundant fruits, unfailing, unforbidden, and on lofty couches. Of a rare creation have we created the houris [beautiful young women], and we have made them ever virgins, dear to their spouses, of equal age with them, for the people of the right hand, a crowd of the former, and a crowd of the latter generations. But the people of the left hand--oh! how wretched shall be the people of the left hand! Amid scorching winds and in scalding water, and in the shadow of a black smoke, not cool, and horrid to behold.

Surah 56, *Al-Waqiah*

From *The Koran*, translated from the Arabic by J.M. Rodwell. (London: B. Quaritch, 1876).

Speak unto the believers that they restrain their eyes and observe continence. Thus will they be more pure. God is well aware of what they do.

And speak to the believing women that they refrain their eyes, and observe continence; and that they display not their ornaments, except those which are external; and that they throw their veils over their bosoms, and display not their ornaments, except to their husbands or their fathers, or their husbands' fathers, or their sons, or their husbands' sons, or their brothers, or their brothers' sons, or their sisters' sons, or their women, or their slaves, or male domestics who have no natural force, or to children who note not women's nakedness. And let them not strike their feet together, so as to discover their hidden ornaments. And be ye all turned to God, O ye Believers! that it may be well with you.

Surah 24, *An Nur*

Hadith

Hadith of Bukhari

From sacred-texts.com. Introduction by Tim Davis (2016)

The Hadith are narratives, stories, reports, and accounts that pertain particularly to the life and actions of the prophet Muhammad. They come from oral tradition and began to be written down after the Prophet's death, but unlike the Qur'ân, occupy a very wide time frame for composition. A small number were recorded during the Umayyad Dynasty (661-750 CE), then they began to proliferate after that. By the ninth century, a collection of over 600,000 Hadiths had been amassed. It is considered a source of authority second only to the Qur'ân, but religion scholars also see them as an evolving part of Islamic tradition. Muslim scholars and jurists have even classified them based upon the opinion of their authenticity or reliability. However, there is often disagreement between Sunni and Shi in regard to the authenticity of particular Hadiths. Many Hadiths often come with their own "isnad," a kind of chain of custody, provenance, support, or sequence of reporting that document the origin and preservation of the sayings. There are also Hadiths that refer to associates of the Prophet and his successors who came from the next generation of the Ummah (community of the faithful) following his death. The Hadith is still used in Muslim jurisprudence and continues to be part of mainstream Muslim tradition today.

Hadith 1:37

Narrated Abu Huraira:
Allah's Apostle said, "Whoever observes fasts during the month of Ramadan out of sincere faith, and hoping to attain Allah's rewards, then all his past sins will be forgiven."

Hadith 1:39

Narrated Al-Bara' (bin 'Azib):
When the Prophet came to Medina, he stayed first with his grandfathers or maternal uncles from Ansar. He offered his prayers facing Baitul-Maqdis (Jerusalem) for sixteen or seventeen months, but he wished that he could pray facing the Ka'ba (at Mecca). The first prayer which he offered facing the Ka'ba was the 'Asr prayer in the company of some people. Then one of those who had offered that prayer with him came out and passed by some people in a mosque who were bowing during their prayers (facing Jerusalem). He said addressing them, "By Allah, I testify that I have prayed with Allah's Apostle facing Mecca (Ka'ba)." Hearing that, those people changed their direction towards the Ka'ba immediately. Jews and the people of the scriptures used to be pleased to see the Prophet facing Jerusalem in prayers but when he changed his direction towards the Ka'ba, during the prayers, they disapproved of it.

Al-Bara' added, "Before we changed our direction towards the Ka'ba (Mecca) in prayers, some Muslims had died or had been killed and we did not know what to say about them (regarding their prayers.) Allah then revealed: And Allah would never make your faith (prayers) to be lost (i.e. the prayers of those Muslims were valid).'" (2:143).

Hadith 1:29

Narrated Al-Ma'rur:
At Ar-Rabadha I met Abu Dhar who was wearing a cloak, and his slave, too, was wearing a similar one. I asked about the reason for it. He replied, "I abused a person by calling his mother names." The Prophet said to me, 'O Abu Dhar! Did you abuse him by calling his mother bad names? You still have some characteristics of ignorance. Your slaves are your brothers and Allah has put them under your command. So whoever has a brother under his command should feed him of what he eats and dress him of what he wears. Do not ask them (slaves) to do things beyond their capacity (power) and if you do so, then help them.'"

Hadith 1:63

Narrated Anas bin Malik:

While we were sitting with the Prophet in the mosque, a man came riding on a camel. He made his camel kneel down in the mosque, tied its foreleg and then said: "Who amongst you is Muhammad?" At that time the Prophet was sitting amongst us (his companions) leaning on his arm. We replied, "This white man reclining on his arm." The man then addressed him, "O Son of 'Abdul Muttalib."

The Prophet said, "I am here to answer your questions." The man said to the Prophet, "I want to ask you something and will be hard in questioning. So do not get angry." The Prophet said, "Ask whatever you want." The man said, "I ask you by your Lord, and the Lord of those who were before you, has Allah sent you as an Apostle to all the mankind?" The Prophet replied, "By Allah, yes." The man further said, "I ask you by Allah, has Allah ordered you to offer five prayers in a day and night (24 hours)?" He replied, "By Allah, Yes." The man further said, "I ask you by Allah, has Allah ordered you to observe fasts during this month of the year (i.e. Ramadan)?" He replied, "By Allah, Yes." The man further said, "I ask you by Allah. Has Allah ordered you to take Zakat (obligatory charity) from our rich people and distribute it amongst our poor people?" The Prophet replied, "By Allah, yes." Thereupon that man said, "I have believed in all that with which you have been sent . . . ."

Hadith 1:437

Narrated 'Abdullah bin 'Umar:

In the life-time of Allah's Apostle the mosque was built of adobes, its roof of the leaves of date-palms and its pillars of the stems of date-palms. Abu Bakr did not alter it. 'Umar expanded it on the same pattern as it was in the lifetime of Allah's Apostle by using adobes, leaves of date-palms and changing the pillars into wooden ones. 'Uthman changed it by expanding it to a great extent and built its walls with engraved stones and lime and made its pillars of engraved stones and its roof of teak wood.

Hadith 3:88

Narrated Anas:

The Prophet saw an old man walking, supported by his two sons, and asked about him. The people informed him that he had vowed to go on foot (to the Ka'ba). He said, "Allah is not in need of this old man's torturing himself," and ordered him to ride.

Narrated Abu Huraira:

The Prophet said, "There was a merchant who used to lend the people, and whenever his debtor was in straitened circumstances, he would say to his employees, 'Forgive him so that Allah may forgive us.' So, Allah forgave him."

Sufi Texts

Rumi

From *The Spiritual Couplets of Rumi,* translated by H.E. Whinfield (1898)

The Monk's Search for a Man

The monk said, "I am searching everywhere for a man
Who lives by the life of the breath of God."
The other said, "Here are men; the bazaar is full;

These are surely men, O enlightened sage!"
The monk said, "I seek a man who walks straight
As well in the road of anger as in that of lust.
Where is one who shows himself a man in anger and lust?
In search of such a one I run from street to street.
If there be one who is a true man in these two states,
I will yield up my life for him this day!"
The other, who was a fatalist, said, "What you seek is rare.
But you are ignorant of the force of the divine decree;
You see the branches, but ignore the root.
We men are but branches, God's eternal decree the root.
That decree turns from its course the revolving sky,
And makes foolish hundreds of planets like Mercury.
It reduces to helplessness the world of devices;
It turns steel and stone to water.
O you who attribute stability to these steps on the road,
You are one of the raw ones; yea, raw, raw!
When you have seen the millstone turning round,
Then, go and see the stream that turns it.
When you have seen the dust rising up into the air,

182

Go and mark the air in the midst of the dust.
You see the kettles of thought boiling over,
Look with intelligence at the fire beneath them.
God said to Job, 'Out of my clemency
I have given a grain of patience to every hair of thine.'
Look not, then, so much at your own patience;
After seeing patience, look to the Giver of patience.
How long will you confine your view to the waterwheel?
Lift up your head and view also the water."

The Soul and the Spirit of Prayer

Sadi's Scroll of Wisdom

From *Sadi's Scroll of Wisdom*, by Arthur N. Wollaston, (1906), at sacred-texts.com . Introduction by Tim Davis (2016)

Sadi was a twelfth-century Persian poet from Shiraz. While a student at Baghdad, he gave up his station to follow a contemplative lifestyle. He developed a following and a reputation for holiness, having made the pilgrimage to Mecca some fourteen times on foot. He was widely traveled but found time to retreat from society for periods of contemplation. Sadi spent his final years living in the cell of a contemplative in the city of Shiraz where he received many who sought his wisdom. His writings on virtue, morality, and mystical thought have been famously preserved by his followers.

IN PRAISE OF GENEROSITY

O soul! whoever spreadeth the table of benevolence
Is famous in the world of liberality.
Generosity will make thee renowned throughout the universe;
Generosity will secure thee happiness.
Beside generosity there is nothing in the world,
Nor is aught more current in any market!
Generosity will be the source of delight;
Generosity will be the harvest of life.
Freshen the heart of the world by generosity;
Fill the globe with the renown of thy generosity.
For ever be steadfast in generosity;
Since the Creator of the soul is beneficent.

IN CONDEMNATION OF PRIDE

Beware, O son! that thou dost not become proud,
Lest fortune thereby slip from thine hands.
Pride on the part of a wise man is not comely;
Sad is such demeanor in the case of a prudent person.
Pride is the habit of the ignorant,
Pride doth not proceed from men of intelligence.
Pride caused the fall of Azazil (the lead angel who became Satan)
And led to his being ensnared in the prison of the accursed.
Whoever is by nature arrogant,
His head is filled with pride beyond imagination.
Pride is the source of adversity,
Pride is the nature of the evil-disposed.
Since thou knowest about pride, why dost thou pursue it?
If thou acts thus, thou doest wrong.

DESCRIPTION OF OBEDIENCE AND WORSHIP

When fortune is a person's slave
His heart is perpetually disposed towards obedience.
It is not fit to turn aside one's head from servitude,
Since fortune is obtainable from obedience.
Happiness is procured from obedience;
The heart becomes illumined from the light of obedience.
If thou girdest thy loins with submission,
Thou wilt open the door of everlasting happiness.
The wise man doth not turn his head from obedience,
Since no excellence is more lofty than obedience.
Keep thine ablutions freshened with the waters of obedience,
So that tomorrow thou may be free as from fire.
Establish thy prayers with sincerity,
So that thou may attain everlasting prosperity.
Enlightenment of soul springs from obedience,
Just as the earth derives light from the sun.
Worship the Creator;
Sit down in the portals of obedience.
If thou make choice to worship the Creator,
Thou wilt be a chieftain in the kingdom of fortune.

Raise thy head and keep not abstinence in thy pocket,
For Paradise is the abode of the abstinent.
Lighten the lamp of thy soul with piety,
That thou may become happy, like the prosperous.
Whoever is clad with the garment of religion
Hath no fear for the trials of the day of judgment.

Al Ghazali

From sacred-texts.com. Introduction by Tim Davis (2016)

Al-Ghazali (1058-1111) was a Persian mystic and philosopher known for rejecting certain Neoplatonic and Aristotelian ideas, such as the world being eternal rather than created. After having a spiritual crisis, he left his position as a professor at the University of Baghdad. He traveled around living a solitary and modest lifestyle. Eventually, in 1096, he made the pilgrimage to the city of Mecca. Shortly afterward he took up the life of a Sufi, and would come to teach others that mysticism is the path to true knowledge of God. He soon saw these practices as allowing the body and soul to be in a state of harmony. Al-Ghazali realized that there is a limit to what one can know on the basis of philosophy and reason. Philosophy deals with what is finite. In order to truly understand the nature of reality and God, he believed one must have an experience that lies beyond reason.

On Sufism

"Sufism is this: that actions should be passing over the Sufi (i.e., being done upon him) which are known to God only, and that he should always be with God in a way that is known to God only."

"Sufism is wholly self-discipline."

"Sufism is, to possess nothing and to be possessed by nothing."

"Sufism is not a system composed of rules or sciences but a moral disposition; i.e., if it were a rule, it could be made one's own by strenuous exertion, and if it were a science, it could be acquired by instruction; but on the contrary it is a disposition, according to the saying, 'Form yourselves on the moral nature of God;' and the moral nature of God cannot be attained either by means of rules or by means of sciences."

"Sufism is freedom and generosity and absence of self-constraint."

"It is this: that God should make thee die to thyself and should make thee live in Him."

"To behold the imperfection of the phenomenal world, nay, to close the eye to everything imperfect in contemplation of Him who is remote from all imperfection--that is Sufism."

"Sufism is control of the faculties and observance of the breaths."

From: The Secret Rose Garden

by Sa'd ud Din Mahmud Shabistari

(13th century Sufi writer)

translated by Florence Lederer (1920)

FREE-WILL

You say, "I myself have Free-will,
For my body is the horse and my soul the rider,
The reins of the body are in the hands of the soul,
The entire direction is given to me."
Oh! foolish one, these are falsehoods and delusions
That come from an illusory existence.
As your essence is nothingness,
How can you have Free-will?
Seeing that your being is one with not-being,
Whence comes this Free-will of yours?
Imagination distributes actions
As in a play or a farce,
For when your actions were planned,
Before your existence,
You were created for a certain purpose,
By the desire of the Truth.
Therefore is man predestined, before his existence,
To certain appointed work.

The honor of man consists of slavery,
In having no share of Free-will.
Of himself man has nothing,
Yet of good and evil God asks him,
Man has no choice, he is under control.
Oh! poor soul, he seems free, yet is a slave.
Give yourself up to the Truth,
For you are helpless in his grasp;
Freedom from self you will find in the All,
And, O Dervish! in the Truth you will find riches